For Theo,
with compliments

Christopher Hitchens

CYPRUS

CYPRUS

Christopher Hitchens

Quartet Books
London Melbourne New York

First published by Quartet Books Limited 1984
A member of the Namara Group
27/29 Goodge Street, London W1P 1FD
Reprinted 1984

British Library Cataloguing in Publication Data

Hitchens, Christopher
  Cyprus.
  1. Cyprus—Politics and government
  I. Title
  956.45'04   DS54.9

  ISBN 0-7043-2436-9

Typeset by MC Typeset, Chatham, Kent
Printed and bound in Great Britain
by Mackays of Chatham Ltd, Kent

This book is for Eleni,
and for Laurence Stern (1929–79)

Contents

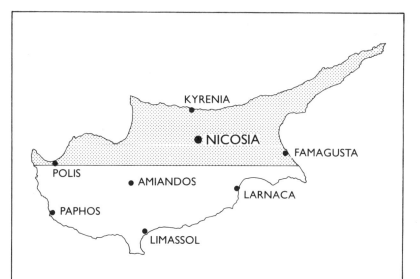

Above: partition of Cyprus suggested in 1957 by the Turkish
Cypriot leader, Dr Fazil Kuchuk, in his pamphlet *The Cyprus
Question: A Permanent Solution*. (The Turkish part is the
shaded area in the north of the island) *Below*: the partition
line as established by the Turkish army in 1974

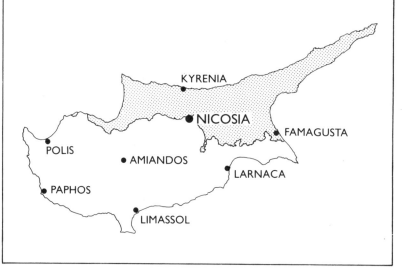

Preface

Ten years ago, the Republic of Cyprus was attacked by one member of NATO and invaded and partitioned by another. Since 1948, and the period of armed truce which that year inaugurated in Europe, no member of either opposing alliance had actually sought to change the boundaries of an existing state. The Soviet Union had sent its troops into Hungary and Czechoslovakia and retained political control over Poland and the other Warsaw Pact nations by its understood readiness to use force. But those nations retain their integrity as countries, whatever political indignities they may endure. The Western powers, also, have agreed to respect existing European borders even when, as in the case of Ireland, one party regards the demarcation as historically unjust.

Only in one case has a member of either post-war bloc succeeded in redrawing the map. Turkey, by its invasion of Cyprus in 1974 and its subsequent occupation of the northern third of the island, has finally (if not legally or morally) created a new political entity. It has done so in the face of much Western criticism, but also with considerable Western assistance. It is commonplace to say that the resulting situation is a threat to peace in the eastern Mediterranean. It is equally commonplace to hear that it has *brought* peace, of a kind, to Cyprus. Both of these opinions, or impressions, miss the point. The first statement would make the island a mere intersection on the graph of differences between Greece and Turkey. The second is an unoriginal echo of Tacitus's '*Ubi solitudinem faciunt, pacem apellant*' – 'They make a desert, and they call it peace.' Tacitus, through the reported speech of Calgacus, was at least attempting to be ironic.

These two pseudo-realist interpretations have to compete in popularity with a third, which might be called the liberal or *bien-pensant* view. It is most pithily summarized by Ms Nancy Crawshaw, at the conclusion of her voluminous but not exhaustive book *The Cyprus Revolt.* Ms Crawshaw, who reported Cyprus for the *Guardian* in the 1950s and 1960s, ends her narrative like this: 'In Cyprus itself the Turkish invasion marked the climax of the struggle for union with Greece which had begun more than one hundred years earlier. The Greek Cypriots had paid dearly in the cause of *enosis*: in terms of human suffering the cost to both communities was beyond calculation.'

Here, pseudo-realism is replaced by pseudo-humanitarianism. We are all (it goes without saying) sorry for the victim. But it is, we very much regret to say, the victim's *fault.*

All these consoling explanations make it easier for those responsible to excuse themselves and for the rest of the world to forget about Cyprus. But such a loss of memory would be unpardonable. It would mean forgetting about the bad and dangerous precedent that has been set by invasion; by a larger power suiting itself by altering geography and demography. It would mean overlooking the aspiration of a European people to make a passage from colonial rule to sovereignty in one generation. And it would mean ignoring an important example, afforded by Cyprus, of the way in which small countries and peoples are discounted or disregarded by the superpowers (and, on occasion, by liberal commentators).

The argument of this book is that the Turkish invasion was *not* 'the climax of the struggle for union with Greece', but the outcome of a careless and arrogant series of policies over which Cypriots had little or no control. The conventional picture, of a dogged and narrow battle of Greek against Turk, has become, with further and better knowledge, simplistic and deceptive.

Only four years after they had painfully achieved independence, the Cypriots became the victims of a superpower design for partition. This partition reflected only the strategic requirements of outside powers, and did not conform to any local needs. The economy of Cyprus, with its distribution of water resources and agriculture, makes partition an absurdity. So does, or did, the distribution of population. And there is certainly no room for two machineries of state, unless at least one of them is imposed by another country. The imposition of partition *necessitated* the setting of Greek against Turk, and Greek against Greek. As I will show, strenuous efforts were made in that direction. They maximized all the possible disadvantages, and led to dire results for Greece and Turkey as well as for Cyprus.

If one were to attempt a series of conjectures on Cyprus, they might read something like this:

1. Cyprus is, by population and by heritage, overwhelmingly Greek. But it has never been part of Greece.

2. Cyprus has a Turkish minority, but was ruled by Turkey for three centuries.

3. The proportion of Greeks to Turks in Cyprus is four to one, approximately the *inverse* of the proportion of mainland Greeks to mainland Turks. The distance between Cyprus and Greece is more than ten times the distance between Cyprus and Turkey.

4. Cyprus is the involuntary host to three NATO armies, none of which has been sufficient to protect it from aggression.

5. The Cypriots are the only Europeans to have undergone colonial rule, guerrilla war, civil war and modern technological war, on their own soil, since 1945.

6. Cyprus is the last real test of British post-imperial policy; a test that has so far resulted in a succession of failures.

7. Cyprus was the site, and the occasion, of perhaps the greatest failure of American foreign policy in post-war Europe.

8. Cyprus was critical in the alternation of military and democratic rule in both Greece and Turkey.

What follows is not designed to make the Cyprus drama appear any simpler. But it is designed to challenge the obfuscations which, by purporting to make it simple, have, often deliberately, made it impossible to understand.

The axis of the book is the summer of 1974; the months of July and August, during which Cyprus was dismembered as an independent republic. I describe how the policies of four countries – Britain, Greece, Turkey and the United States – contributed to the 1974 catastrophe. I then describe how that catastrophe affected, in their turn, those four states. It will be for the reader to judge whether, in the light of what follows, it is fair to blame the current plight of Cyprus on the shortcomings of its inhabitants.

Christopher Hitchens
Washington D.C. January 1984

Acknowledgements

In almost a decade of engagement with Cyprus, both as a country and as a 'problem', I have incurred a lifetime of debt. My thanks are due to the late, first President of the Republic, His Beatitude Archbishop Makarios III, and to the Turkish Cypriot leader Mr Rauf Denktash, for their hospitality and for the generosity with which they gave up their time to my questioning. The current President of the Republic, HE Spiros Kyprianou, was no less helpful to me. Among Greek Cypriot party leaders, I must single out Dr Vassos Lyssarides and his wife Barbara for my gratitude; also Mr Glafkos Clerides, Dr Takis Hadjidimitriou, Mr Tassos Papadopoulos and Mr Andreas Ziartides. On the Turkish Cypriot side, I am indebted to Mr Alpay Durduran, Mr Osker Ozgur, the late Dr Fazil Kuchuk, Dr Ahmed Midat Berberoglu and Dr Kenan Atakol.

Cyprus is fortunate in having an outspoken press and many talented commentators, enthusiasts and authorities. To my friends Andreas Christophides, George and Androulla Lanitis, Michael Attalides and Chysostomos Pericleos, as well as my friends Akay Camal, Mustapha Adiloglu and Oktay Oksuzoglu, thanks are due for many evenings of rare Cypriot warmth as well as many moments of enlightenment. Costa Kyrris and George Georghallides of the Cyprus Research Centre were helpful and patient. Polyvios Polyviou is a lawyer's lawyer. Stella Soulioti is a scholar's scholar. His Excellency Cvieto Job, Ambassador of Yugoslavia, is a diplomat's diplomat.

In Greece, I was fortunate enough to have lengthy discussions with Prime Minister Andreas Papandreou, as well as with the Leader of the Opposition Evangelos Averoff-Tosizza. Leonidas Kyrkos, Constantine Kalligas, Dr John Pezmazoglou,

Nicos Kyriazides, General George Koumanakos, Admiral Paizis-Paradelis and Christos Papoutsakis helped me to a better understanding of modern Greek politics and history.

In Turkey, Orhan Kologlu, Nuri Colakoglu and Metin Munir were good to me, as were Savas Akat and Senator Besim Ustunel. The difficult political conditions in today's Turkey make it necessary to thank many others without giving their names.

In London, where much of the institutional memory of the Cyprus question is still to be found, I benefited from the experience of Lord Caradon, Sir David Hunt, the Hon. C.M. Woodhouse, Costa Carras, Christopher Price, Leslie Finer, Osman Turkay, Peter Loizos, Edward Mortimer, David Tonge, Robert Stephens, Peter Thompson, Brigadier Michael Harbottle, Lord Bethell and the late Lord Bradwell.

In Washington D.C., where this book was completed, and elsewhere in the United States, I was able to draw on the experience of Professors Van Coufoudakis, John O. Iatrides, Theodore Couloumbis and John Koumoulides. John Brademas, a distinguished former Congressman and House Majority Whip, now distinguished President of New York University, has been generous to me since our first meeting in 1975. Nicholas X. Rizopoulos, an exacting critic and the director of the Lehrman Institute in New York City, was kind enough to make me an associate of the institute and to include me in several round tables where I could test the ideas of this book against superior firepower. Seymour Hersh gave me encouragement and guidance. Kenneth Egan, of the Hellenic American Development Alliance, was an unfailing friend and guided my faltering steps through modern technology. The late Laurence Stern, still so genuinely and deeply missed all over Washington, was present at this book's conception. Present at its delivery was Elias P. Demetracopoulos, whose encyclo-paedic knowledge of Greece, of Capitol Hill and of other areas of human weakness is matched only by his unselfish readiness to share what he has learned. For reasons which I am afraid that the book makes all too clear, few official Americans to whom I spoke were willing to be quoted.

Portions of this book appeared as 'work in progress' in a

number of magazines, and I'm grateful to Anthony Howard and Bruce Page of the *New Statesman*, Victor Navasky of the *Nation*, Alexander Chancellor of the *Spectator*, Perry Anderson and Robin Blackburn of the *New Left Review*, Tamar Jacoby of the *New York Times*, Robert Kaiser of the *Washington Post*, Steve Wasserman of the *Los Angeles Times* and Robert Silvers of the *New York Review of Books*.

It is conventional to say that none of the above-mentioned bears any responsibility for what follows. I make this time-honoured disclaimer as a hypocrite. Many friends and colleagues are, in effect, co-responsible for any merit these chapters have. Errors and omissions are mine alone.

Cyprus

Introduction

> The struggle of man against power is the struggle of
> memory against forgetting.
> Milan Kundera

There is a sense in which all of us are prisoners of knowledge.
Most people who think at all about the island of Cyprus will rely
on two well-imprinted ideas of it. The first is that of an insular
paradise; the birthplace of Aphrodite; the perfect beaches and
mountains; the olive groves; the gentle people and the
wine-dark sea. The second is that of a 'problem' too long on the
international agenda; of an issue somehow incorrigible and
insoluble but capable of indefinite relegation. In some
accounts, the quaintness and the antiquity of the first impression reinforce the intractability of the second. Cyprus becomes a
curiosity – melancholy perhaps, but tolerable to outsiders and
lacking in urgency. Meanwhile, there is still the vineyard and
the siesta; the cool interiors and the village raconteur to delight
and distract the visitor. The Victorian Bishop Heber, writing of
another island, gave us the fatuous stock phrase, 'Where every
prospect pleases and only man is vile.' In Cyprus, this duality
was expressed most vividly by Lawrence Durrell in his beautiful
but patronizing memoir *Bitter Lemons*.

In a fashion, I envy those who can continue to see Cyprus in
this way. But I am the captive of a certain limited knowledge of
the place. The eastern Mediterranean affords few better
evenings than the one provided by the dusk in Nicosia, the
capital. The Pentadactylos mountains, so named for the
five-knuckled and fist-like peak which distinguishes the range,
turn from a deep purple to a stark black outline against the sun.

To the newcomer, the sight is a stirring one. But to many of my friends, the mountains at that hour take on the look of a high and forbidding wall. Beyond the peaks are their old homes and villages, and the charm of the sunset is dissolved into an impression of claustrophobia.

By day, if one takes the promenade down the busiest shopping street in town, there comes a point where the advertisements, the bars and the inducements simply run out. There is no point, for most people, in proceeding further. They retrace their steps, and find another turning with more promise. But if you walk the extra few hundred yards, you find yourself in one of the modern world's political slums. A tangle of barbed wire, a zariba of cement-filled oil drums, a row of charred and abandoned shops and houses. Only the weeds and nettles justify the designation 'Green Line'. This line, which in many places follows the old Venetian wall enclosing Nicosia, marks the furthest point of the Turkish advance in 1974. Soldiers in fatigues warn against the taking of photographs. The red crescent flag of Turkey confronts the blue and white of Greece and the green, yellow and white of Cyprus. Late at night, leaving a taverna, you can hear the Turkish soldiers shouting their bravado across the line. It is usually bluff, but nobody who remembers their arrival will ever quite learn to laugh it off. Continue to walk along the line, in daylight, and there are reminders at every turn. Here, almost concealed behind the Archbishopric, is the Museum of National Struggle. Entering, one finds the memorabilia of a five-year guerrilla war against the British crown – symbolized most acutely by the replica gallows and gibbet that made the United Kingdom famous in so many of her former possessions. A few streets away, on the road back to the city centre and so low down on the wall that you miss it if you are not looking, is set the memorial to Doros Loizou, one of the many Greek Cypriots murdered by the Greek junta in its effort to annex the island in 1974. Proceed in the same direction and you come eventually to the Ledra Palace Hotel, once counted among the most spacious and graceful in the Levant. Its battered but still splendid shape now houses the soldiers of the United Nations: Swedes, Quebecois, Finns, Austrians. A parched no man's land, perhaps half a mile wide at this point, separates the two barricades. No Cypriot, Greek or Turkish, may cross this line. The Venetian wall bulges outwards near this spot and the Turkish flag, complete with armed Turkish guard, commands the roundabout where the national telephone exchange sits, and the road where the National Museum and the National Theatre lie. Drivers and pedestrians seem never to look up at the only Turks they are allowed to see. A desolate Armenian cemetery and a burned-out bookshop complete the picture. But all of these details, smudges on the Cypriot panorama, require a slight detour which nobody much cares to make. The roads which lead to them do not lead anywhere else. You do not have to see them, but I always do.

Once having acquired these spectacles, enabling (or compelling) one to see both aspects of the island, it is impossible to take them off again. A visit to the marvellous mosaics of Paphos, which offer a pictorial history of the discovery of wine and a skilfully worked rendering of the myth of Pyramus and Thisbe, is full of pitfalls. One has to recall the Turkish shells that fell on the mosaic floor and the heartrending labour involved in remaking the pattern so that newcomers would not see the difference. In the exquisite village of Peristerona, which boasts an ancient painted church and a fine but now locked and deserted mosque, there is an ugly litter of improvised new buildings. This is not a result of the lust for vulgar development that so disfigures the rest of the Mediterranean. It is the hastily erected shelter for refugees from nearby Greek villages. They have been evicted from their homes and orchards, but at midday or evening they can still see the outlines of their old dwellings against the sky, and there is some comfort, as well as some pain, in the proximity. The invisible but still palpable line of division runs here, too. There is no village or town, however far from that line, which does not pay an indemnity to it with improvised refugee housing, and with memories.

It is in conversation with Cypriots themselves, however, that the even more serious wounds inflicted on Cyprus become apparent. The most casual inquiry – such as, 'Where are you from?' or 'Do you have a family?' – can be enough to induce a torrent of grievance or of grief. Sometimes, depending on the nationality of the listener, the litany may be historic – usually beginning with the many broken promises of the British colonial administration. If, like myself, the listener actually is British, this recitation is accompanied by denials of any but warm feelings towards the other island race, and the denial is made good by the inflexible refusal to allow the foreigner to pay for his own drink. The largest overseas Cypriot community is in London, and most families have a relative there. But the relationship between the two countries, though friendly, has been one of disappointment. 'Britain promised us. . .', 'The British gave their word. . .' – I can do it from memory now and, worse, I know that the complaint is substantially justified.

At least such discussion is political; and to that extent, detached and objective. The hard listening comes if your companions are from the Karpass peninsula, from Bellapaix, from Famagusta, from Lapithos, from Morphou or from Kyrenia. With eyes half closed they can tell you of their lost homes, their orchards, their farms and their animals. After ten years of expulsion and eviction it is dawning on even the most naïve and trusting of them that this separation may be forever. Attachment to land and property, and sense of place, is very deep-rooted in Cyprus. The wrenching out of those roots has been unusually painful. A Cypriot may bid adieu to his old village and set off, as many have done, to seek prosperity in America, in England, in the Gulf or the Levant. But the village or the town remains his or hers, and is often reflected in the patronymic (Zodiates, Paphitis and so on). In the end, this says, there can be a homecoming. But there is a difference between being an exile and being a refugee, and this difference is sinking in. It is the estrangement of one-third of the island, the alienation of it in perpetuity by an invader, that is shocking and unbearable.

Some have even harsher stories to relate. I have heard women describe the rape inflicted by the Turkish army, and describe it as if it were yesterday. Virginity is still highly prized in Cyprus, and the loss of it before marriage, let alone the loss of it to an uncaring invading soldier, is a disaster beyond words or remedy. I have a vivid memory of watching the filmed interviews with rape victims which were accepted as part of the archive of evidence by members of the European Commission for Human Rights during their 1976 investigation. The young women had serious difficulty in looking into the camera, but they told their stories with a certain stoic resignation, as if they had nothing more to lose. The term they employed for the violation itself was the Greek word *katéstrepse* in its passive verbal form – as in, 'then he ruined me' or 'then they ruined me again'. Ever since, I have avoided that stale journalistic usage, 'the rape of Cyprus'.

Worse than the nostalgia for home, or the shame of desecration, is the moment when Cypriots say that one of their own is 'among the missing'. At this, a sort of pool of silence forms around the speaker. Just under two thousand Greek Cypriots are still unaccounted for since the 1974 events, and that is a horrifying number out of a total population of less than 650,000. Many of them, no doubt, perished in battle and were never found. Still others, we must assume, were mutilated beyond recognition or torn apart by scavenging animals. But the fact remains that many were photographed and identified while held prisoner by the Turkish army, and have never been seen again. I have traced one or two of these cases myself, and the trail goes cold some time after the shutter closed on that familiar, modern picture of the young men sitting in the sun, on the bare ground, hands behind their heads, under armed guard. The surviving relatives remain prisoners of that memory, of that photograph, for the rest of their lives. Even in an island less reverent about family ties, the length of the sentence would be unimaginably long.

The injuries done to Cyprus are rendered more poignant (or, according to some Anglo–American sources, less so) by the fact that it is an outwardly modern and European society. Its efficiency, its canny use of tourist resources and its good communications give it a special standing in the Levant. Many battle-weary correspondents and businessmen employ it as a sort of recreational decompression-chamber after the exigencies of the Egyptian telephone system or the carnage of Beirut. It has a free press, a functioning party system, a simple visa requirement and a prosperous façade. It is not disfigured by any gross extremes of wealth or poverty, though there is a certain ostentation among the new-rich class of hotel owners and tourist operators. English is a *lingua franca.*

Yet the geography of the island has ensured that it cannot become a mere tourist and 'offshore' haven. If you take your skis up to the mountain resort of Troodos, you will not be able to avoid seeing the golf-ball-shaped monitoring station which sits on the top of Mount Olympus and sucks at the airwaves of the Middle East. If you drive from Nicosia to Paphos, or take the other direction and head for Ayia Napa or the Paralimni coast (just south of that strangest of sights, the deserted modern city of Famagusta guarded by Turkish troops), you will have to pass through the British base areas. They cover a total of ninety-nine square miles, under a remarkable treaty which the Cyprus government does not have the right to alter or terminate. From these bases, spy planes with British and American markings overfly the neighbouring countries. Within the purlieus of these 'Sovereign Base Areas', a mock-heroic attempt has been made to re-create the deadly atmosphere of Aldershot or Camberley. Rows of suburban married quarters are in evidence, ranged along streets named after Nelson and Drake and Montgomery. Sprinklers play on trimmed lawns. Polo and cricket and the Church of England are available. And a radio station brings the atmosphere of the English Sunday morning to Cyprus, with record requests, quiz shows and news of engagements and weddings. These chintzy reminders of the former colonial mastery are not much resented in themselves. Perhaps paradoxically, the Cypriots most resent the *failure* of Britain to assert itself in 1974. But that is for a later chapter.

Conversation with Greek Cypriots, any one in three of whom may turn out to be a refugee in his own country, takes on an even more sombre note when they ask, 'And have you visited the other side?' Everywhere can be seen restaurants, bars, hotels and taxi firms which are named after old businesses in the north. The 'Tree of Idleness' café, beloved of Lawrence Durrell in Bellapaix, is now re-established by its old owner on a hill overlooking Nicosia. Then there is everything from Famagusta Apartments to Kyrenia Car Hire. Official road signs still give the direction and mileage of these lost locations. As I said, those roads do not lead anywhere. But for the foreign journalist or diplomat they do converge on the checkpoint at the old Ledra Palace Hotel. Here, after an encounter with an Ottoman-type officialdom, it is possible to negotiate permission to visit the Turkish-held sector, known since November 1983 as the Turkish State of North Kibris.

In a decade or so, if things go on as they are, it may well be possible for a visitor ignorant of history to arrive and to imagine that there have always been two states on the island. So thorough has been the eradication of Greekness in the north that, if one were not the prisoner of one's knowledge, one could relax very agreeably. This is the most beautiful part of Cyprus and the Turkish Cypriots are every bit as courteous and hospitable as their Greek fellows. But their 'state' is built upon an awful negation. Every now and then, usually in the old quarter of Turkish Nicosia, one can see the outline of a Greek sign, imperfectly painted over. Otherwise, every street and place name has been changed and, unlike the situation in the Republic, there are no bilingual signs. Kyrenia has become Girne. Famagusta is Gazi Magusa. Lapithos is Lapta. The currency has been changed to permit only Turkish mainland money to circulate. Even the clocks have been put back one hour, so that the north of Cyprus beats time, literally as well as metaphorically, with Anatolia.

To cross the line is to enter a looking-glass world. The 1974 invasion is known as the 'peace operation'. Cyprus is called, even in English-language official documents, 'Kibris'. Busts of Kemal Ataturk adorn every village square. Monuments to the valour of the Turkish army are everywhere, as are more palpable reminders in the shape of thousands of Turkish soldiers. They are marked off from the indigenous population not only by their uniforms and their fatigues, but by the cast of their features, which is unmistakably Anatolian.

In the whole atmosphere of the place there is something of protesting too much. The square-jawed Ataturk busts are, perhaps, a little too numerous and obtrusive to be a sign of real confidence. The clumsy denials of the Hellenic heritage of the island – symbolized by the conversion of churches into mosques and the neglect and pillage of antiquities – shows the same mixture of the superiority and the inferiority complex which is characteristic of Turkish and Turkish Cypriot claims.

Again, the visitor can be spared much of this. A visit to Bellapaix (whose name remains unaltered except by one consonant) is on every traveller's agenda. The splendid abbey still stands, overlooking the glacis of the Kyrenia range as it descends to the sea. The architectural core of the village thus remains intact, and the little lanes go sloping away from the square as before. In the area just up the hill, mainland Turks and other foreigners compete for newly built villas and a vicarious share in Durrell's long-dissipated 'atmosphere'. When I first saw Bellapaix, it was still Greek. The Turkish army held it under occupation and was suggesting to the inhabitants in numerous ways that they might be happier elsewhere. Certainly they were made to feel unhappy where they were. They needed permission to visit the town, to till their fields, to post letters or to receive visitors. It was only with extreme difficulty that I was allowed to talk to them unsupervised. When attrition failed, the stubborn remainder were simply expelled. Now, the inhabitants are Turkish villagers: Cypriots from the south. I paid a call on them some years later, with a colleague who knew them well and who had, since her last visit, made a special trip to their old home. The Bellapaix Turks hail in the main from Mari, a dusty and undistinguished hamlet off the Limassol road. My friend brought them photographs of the village, which they had not seen for several years, since the 'population exchange' of 1974–5. The effect when she produced the pictures in the coffee-shop was extraordinary. Men ran to fetch relatives and friends; a circle formed in less time than it takes to set down. The snapshots were passed around endlessly – 'Look, some-one's put a new window in old Mehmet's house' – 'There's a lick of paint on the old store.' The *mukhtar* of the village treated us to coffee and drinks; our efforts to share the bill were (as always in Cyprus) regarded as just this side of a grave insult. We eventually had to leave, because of the curfew that falls along the border just after dusk. But we were pressed to stay until the very last moment. These people, living in a village which is coveted above all others by tourists and outsiders, were actually nostalgic for the shabby but homely Mari. Yet an effort of the conscious memory is required to remember a time before partition and separation. The children born in Bellapaix will be brought up without knowledge of Greek Cypriots, but will hear endless official propaganda abut their mendacity and cruelty. Only a few miles away, the Greek Cypriot children of the Mari district will hear tales of the Turkish invasion and of the *dies irae* of 1974. And the talking classes of the advanced countries will assume, as they were intended to, that 'the Turks and the Greeks can't get on together'. In order to criticize this trite and cynical view, which is the psychological counterpart of partition, one has to wage a battle against amnesia. This, in turn, means viewing the history of Cyprus not as a random series of local and atavistic disturbances, but as a protracted, uneven and still incomplete movement for self-determination (or, to put it in a more old-fashioned way, for freedom).

At certain times of day, and at particular bends in the road or curves of the shore, Cyprus is still so lovely that it takes you by the throat. But, when I try to explain the disaster of 1974 to some indifferent politician or smug diplomat, I find myself getting obscurely irritated when they say, as if to palliate the situation, that, 'Of course it's such a shame – and such a beautiful island too.' I have stood on Othello's tower in Famagusta, and climbed to the peak of St Hilarion, and loafed in Kyrenia harbour, and traced the coast of the Karpass peninsula and the hills and coves around Pyrgos. I have drunk the soup after the midnight service of Greek Cypriot Easter, and celebrated Bayram with the Turks. I cut out and kept Sir Harry Luke's 1908 tribute to the island when I first read it:

The peculiar charm possessed by the remnants of the Latin East, that East which knew the rule of Crusading lords and the magnificence of Frankish merchant princes, is of a rare and subtle kind, the offspring of oriental nature and medieval Western art. It lies, if the attempt to define so elusive a thing may be allowed, in Gothic architecture blending with Saracenic beneath a Mediterranean sky, in the courts of ruined castles overgrown with deep green cypresses, in date palms rearing their stately crowns above some abbey's traceried cloisters, in emblazoned flamboyant mansions of golden sandstone warmed and illumined, as they could never be in the West, by the glow of an Eastern sun.

Rereading that passage now, I find it overwritten and sentimental. I am condemned to see all those aspects of Cyprus through the prism of their desecration. They have been spoiled for me and – more crucially – ruined for the Cypriots. Othello's tower is within sight of the empty waste of the city of Varosha. St Hilarion is in a military zone. Pyrgos can be reached only by skirting a fortified enclave and passing through a napalmed village. The Karpass has been subjected to a clearance and repopulated by colonists. And I am also doomed to the knowledge that Sir Harry Luke, like so many colonial chroniclers of his time, loved the country and tolerated the people. To the end of his days, he despised any manifestations of political turbulence among the Cypriots, and regarded the island as a fiefdom of Great Britain.

Even from this perspective, I have still had the privilege of coming to know and to love another people. I believe that I can be objective about the politics of Cyprus, but I most certainly cannot be indifferent or dispassionate. I have tried to preserve this distinction in the following pages, where I argue that the Cypriots are not, as many believe, the chief authors of their own misfortunes. I believe that I may tell a truer story if I admit at once to a sense of outrage which Durrell and his emulators have been spared.

I Hammer or Anvil?

The kingdom has from all time had a variety of masters.
It would be tedious to relate all its vicissitudes.
Giralamo Dandini, *Excerpta Cypria:*
Materials for a History of Cyprus, 1596

When the Turkish army stormed into Cyprus in the summer of 1974, it put an end to the only period of independence and self-government, however qualified, that the island had ever enjoyed. There had been almost no time in the preceding millennia when Cyprus could really be described as having been autonomous, and no ruler since 1191 had spoken Greek – the language of the overwhelming majority – until independence in 1960. None the less, historians and scholars have had little problem in identifying a Cypriot identity. For centuries, the national genius lay in adaptation, in the business of surviving the next wave of conquerors and usurpers. One can hear the Cypriots muttering, as Byzantium succeeds Rome and Venice replaces the Franks, that, 'this, too, will pass'. That is not to say that their history is one of unbroken servitude or, worse, servility. They took such advantage as they could of interregna, of divisions among their masters, and of weaknesses in the structure or polity of neighbouring states. But these revenges and upsurges were essentially those of a small people. The Cypriots were, above all, conditioned by geography. Their favourable position, within such easy reach of Syria, Turkey and Egypt, has often been more of a curse than a boon – a problem that persists up to the present day. But the complexity and variety of Cypriot history cannot efface, any more than could its numerous owners and rulers, one striking fact. The island has been, since the Bronze Age, unmistakably Greek. It

is possible to write this simple sentence, so fraught by later
controversy, with some confidence. During the second millen-
nium before Christ, Cyprus was settled by Achaean Greeks.
Earlier arrivals, from Syria, Cilicia and Anatolia, were of
uncertain provenance and were in any case superseded, over
time, by this one. Previous traces, of interest to the archaeologist, are suggestive of Minoan, Mycenaen, Syrian, Hittite and
other influences. But, even where they are conclusive, they are
episodic and incomplete. The records of antiquity, whether
inscribed on ceramic, mosaic or funerary objects, confirm the
Hellenic character of the island from that time forward.

One says Hellenic rather than Helladic, because Cyprus
could not concern itself directly or consistently with the
happenings on what we might now call the Greek mainland. A
certain 'Greekness' infused the island all the same – the cult of
Aphrodite had its headquarters in Cyprus (as well as its links to
the Astarte cult in the Near East) and the Cypriot poet Stasinos
is claimed as the son-in-law of Homer. Since it was the
judgement of Paris which precipitated the Trojan war, it can
fairly be said that Cypriot mythology is indissoluble from the
Greek. These things may not seem to bear very heavily on the
twentieth century and its less glamorous feuds, but the shaping
of a national consciousness depends on continuity, and the
Cypriot line of descent, passionately affirmed up to the present,
can be attested by disinterested research. Although it served in
many ways as a Levantine melting-pot and entrepôt, although
Phoenician influence is marked, and although the Cypriot
dialect is distinctive even to this day, the Greek stamp was set
on the island when recorded history began.

A glance at the map shows the tempting and vulnerable
position of Cyprus. In the remaining years before Christ it was
counted as a part of Assyria, Persia, the empire of Alexander,
the Hellenistic state of Egypt, Ptolemaic Egypt, and the Roman
Empire. Under that empire it was for some time counted as a
province of Syria. In the interstices of these dynastic and
imperial shifts, in which it was treated as a chattel, Cyprus
managed on more than one occasion to generate the leadership
and energy needed for revolt. It took part in the Ionian
rebellion against Persia, but was so severely punished for its

impudence that it found itself contributing ships to the Persian fleet at the later battle of Salamis. Under King Evagoras there was a breathing space in which temporary unity among the Cypriot city kingdoms was the unstable guarantee of independence. The slaying of Evagoras, the return of the Persian satraps, the triumph of Alexander and the rapid posthumous deliquescence of his empire, all robbed the Cypriots of the ability to be masters in their own house. There is a certain apposite irony in the fact that the most famous Cypriot of antiquity, Zeno of Kition, was born in this period. His foundation of the Stoic school of philosophy must have seemed the only fitting world view.

As recently as the nineteenth century, Cyprus was considered as a possible national home for the Jews (Theodor Herzl bargained earnestly for it with the British cabinet) and as a part of Greater Syria (the emblem of the Syrian 'National Socialist' party makes Cyprus the star in its crescent). Cyprus was also, briefly but importantly, one of the last staging posts of the British Empire and was described by a minister of the British crown, as late as 1954, as a colony which could 'never' expect its independence. So it is scarcely irrelevant, in considering the modern Cypriot case, to keep in mind how deeply rooted is its history of subordination. The easiest way of establishing this point is by means of a chart. (See Chronological Table of Events on pages 167–79.)

Two critical points emerge from the later section of that chronicle. First, Cyprus was the only part of Europe to be a part of a modern European empire. It was held as a colony, not so much for its own sake as to guarantee other colonial dispensations in Egypt, Palestine and India. But it was also governed as a colony itself. This aspect of British policy has been insufficiently stressed – it was anomalous from the beginning, but after 1945 it became simply absurd. The continuation of such a misguided and reactionary programme necessitated a second policy, no less calamitous. Turkey, whose undistinguished stewardship of the island (1571–1878) had been terminated by Britain in the first place, had to be encouraged to view Cyprus as a lost possession. There was justice in this only to the extent that the Turkish Sultan had been somewhat cheated by

Disraeli in the first instance. (Gladstone described the 1878 Cyprus Convention [which embodied spurious guarantees for the Sultan against Tsarist oppression] as 'an act of duplicity not surpassed and rarely equalled in the annals of nations'.) But the Anglo–Turkish *entente*, which was to emerge during the 1950s, was in reality a double negative; a manoeuvre between two countries both of which had used the island without troubling to gain the consent of its inhabitants.

This book is not a history of Cyprus. It is an attempt to explain the forces which brought about the current disastrous situation there. The easiest way in which to do this is to examine the island – the anvil – from three points of view: the Greek, the Turkish and the Anglo–American. The perspective in which both sides now view the problem will then become clearer, as I hope will the context in which ancient rivalries have been exploited for much more modern purposes.

Cyprus and *Enosis*

To most people, the fact that islands like Crete and Rhodes are Greek is a fact almost of nature. It is often forgotten that the emergence of modern Greece has been a long, costly and bloody process. The method of nation-building has a name – *enosis*. As the Greek word for 'union', it is most famous as the slogan under which the Greek Cypriots fought the British occupier. But it has a longer history.

After the Turkish Sultan acknowledged Greek independence in 1830, which it took him nine years of exceedingly cruel and savage fighting to do, the emergent kingdom consisted only of central Greece and the Peloponnese and Cycladic islands. The Treaties of Adrianople and London left Thessaly, Attica, parts of Crete, the Ionian islands, all of Macedonia and Thrace and Samos and the Dodecanese out of account or, as Greek nationalists put it, 'unredeemed'. Cyprus was an unimaginable distance away, although it had supported the 1821 Greek revolution with money and volunteers and although the Turkish authorities had, by way of example, hanged the Greek Orthodox Archbishop of the island in public. (His two surviving nephews escaped the island and became lieutenant-generals in the Greek war of independence.) Not all of the remaining Greek-speaking territories, however, were under Ottoman control. The Ionian islands had been British-ruled since 1815, and in 1858 William Ewart Gladstone visited them and recommended they be ceded, along with their devotedly Hellenic inhabitants, to Greece. Most of Thessaly became Greek in 1881. Crete, after a battle which deserves the overworked designation 'epic', managed to remove the Turks in 1898 and finally became part of Greece in 1913 as a result of Turkish and Bulgarian defeats in the Balkan wars, which brought much of Epirus, Macedonia and Thrace under Greek control. In the meantime, Italy seized Rhodes and the Dodecanese islands from the Ottoman Empire in 1912. They were not to accomplish *enosis* until after the Second World War, and then only because Turkey had been compromised by her wartime neutrality, while Greece had sacrificed heavily for the Allied cause.

In this gradual, painful process of accretion, Cyprus was excluded. Turkey, Britain and Greece had interests there, though the Greek interest was emotional rather than strategic. As Britain had its Philhellenes, so Greece had its Anglophiles. The British gift of the Ionian islands was considered noble and altruistic, while its later stewardship over Cyprus was thought preferable to Turkish suzerainty and – on the available precedents – a likely prelude to eventual *enosis*. This helps to explain why it took the Greek Cypriots so long to revolt against British colonial rule.

There were, in point of fact, three separate and well documented occasions on which the British flirted with the *enosis* idea. The first, and in Cypriot memory the most indelible, was in 1907. Winston Churchill visited the island as Colonial Secretary and received the customary delegation beseeching union with Greece. He responded:

I think it only natural that the Cypriot people, who are of Greek descent, should regard their incorporation with what may be called their mother country as an ideal to be earnestly, devoutly and fervently cherished. Such a feeling is

an example of the patriotic devotion which so nobly
characterizes the Greek nation. . . I say that the views which
have been put forward are views which His Majesty's
Government do not refuse to regard with respect.

This pregnant observation was more widely quoted (by Greeks)
than its codicil, which reads, 'The opinion held by the Muslim
population of the island, that the British occupation of Cyprus
should not lead to the dissolution of the Ottoman Empire . . . is
one which His Majesty's Government are equally bound to
regard with respect.'

'Equally bound.' This was not the last time that the Cypriot
majority was to be told that some grand prior commitment
impeded its right (inalienable, of course, in principle) to
self-determination. Seven years later, the British and Ottoman
empires were at war, and nobody sought with greater energy
'the dissolution of the Ottoman Empire' than Winston Churchill. In pursuit of that objective the British cabinet, in the person
of Sir Edward Grey, offered Cyprus to Greece on 16 October
1915. If the Greek government of the day had not been headed
by a timorous and rather pro-German monarch in the shape of
King Constantine I – who was married to the sister of the Kaiser
– the offer (which involved a Greek pledge to help Serbia as its
quid pro quo) might well have been accepted. By the time that
the republican Eleftherios Venizelos had become Prime Minister in 1917, Greece was already committed to the Allies in any
case and the offer, now otiose, was not repeated. But the
Cypriots could hardly be blamed for construing it as an implicit
admission that their claims were justifiable, if not justified.

Once Turkey had been defeated (and while Greece was
distracted elsewhere by its disastrous and opportunistic Asia
Minor campaign of 1919–22) British rule on the island reverted
to a routine of classic colonial stupor. A book published in 1918
by Captain C.W.J. Orr and entitled *Cyprus under British Rule*
gives an impression of dull-witted administration that is
undoubtedly harsher than its gallant and decent author can
have intended.

The most obvious injustice imposed on Cyprus was the
annual payment of the Tribute; a large sum exacted by the

British Treasury in order to pay the debts of the Sultan of Turkey under the provisions of the 1878 Cyprus Convention. It could be doubted, as Captain Orr politely put it,

> whether the British government has been justified in making the payment due to the Porte under the Cyprus Convention a charge on the Cyprus revenues, or whether, after assuming by treaty with Turkey the responsibility for administering the island – *an arrangement to which the inhabitants of Cyprus were in no way a party* – there was any justification for the British government making this payment a charge on the island revenues. [italics mine]

The Tribute, which was not paid during British hostilities with Turkey during the First World War, was actually reimposed in 1923, on the preposterous grounds that Cyprus, as a successor of the Ottoman Empire, had to shoulder her share of the Ottoman debt. Thus, while new nations were being conceived and created at Versailles, Cyprus remained a possession as it had done for centuries past.

The British are proud of their record of varying unwanted domination with enlightened government. In the person of Sir Ronald Storrs, Governor of Cyprus between 1926 and 1932, this variation is manifest in its most irritating form. Sir Ronald's memoir, *Orientations*, which records his friendship with Lawrence of Arabia, and other demonstrations of his breadth of mind, contains the following luminous sentence: 'The Greekness of the Cypriots is, in my opinion, indisputable. A man is of the race which he passionately feels himself to be.'

Sir Ronald did, in fact, secure the abolition of the Tribute, which was replaced by a levy on Cyprus towards the cost of imperial defence. But when, in 1931, large-scale pro-*enosis* agitation broke out on the island, all ideas of enlightenment and tolerance were abandoned. The display of the Greek flag was forbidden. All political parties were banned. Ten important communal leaders, including the Bishops of Kition and Kyrenia, were deported from the island for life. Two thousand Cypriots were jailed. A huge collective fine was imposed to pay for damage done by the rioters, which included the burning of

Government House. The press was censored even more
severely than before. In fact, all the dreary arsenal of colonial
rule was deployed. At the time, Greece was in a politically
exhausted condition and although there were protests and,
from Venizelos, a prophetic suggestion that Britain grant
partial independence rather than *enosis*, it was felt that all
dissent from that quarter could be ignored.

There were to be two further occasions on which the British
authorities gave implicit recognition to the validity of the *enosis*
demand. In late 1940, when Britain and Greece were the only
two countries in Europe still resisting Fascism, and while the
Greek army was still triumphantly repulsing Mussolini's invasion, there was a renewed enthusiasm among Cypriots for the
Hellenic cause. Sir Michael Palairet, the British ambassador in
Athens, recommended that the island be ceded to Greece on
simple grounds of cementing Anglo–Greek solidarity. He was
seconded in this by Edward Warner and Pierson Dixon of the
Middle East department of the Foreign Office. These men
proposed that Cyprus be swapped for permanent naval facilities
at Suda Bay in Crete. Pro-Turkish officials in the Foreign Office
overruled the idea. They did so in the vain hope that a
postponement of Greek claims in Cyprus and the Dodecanese
islands would help bring about a pro-British policy in Turkey.
Turkey got its way here, as it had in Syria before the war and for
the same reasons. (See pages 153–4.) But it remained, until
February 1945, obstinately neutral and often neutral with a
pro-Axis inclination.

Later in the war, after the capture of Athens and the invasion
of Crete by overwhelming Nazi forces, the Greek government
in exile inquired tactfully whether it might be permitted to
station itself in Cyprus. Here, it said, was the only free part of
the Greek world. Would it not be appropriate to raise the flag
of resistance there, rather than in Cairo where the British had
suggested they base themselves? The reply contained all the
imagination of the colonial bureaucrat. Such a step, the Greeks
were informed, might offend His Majesty's loyal Muslim
subjects. Yet again, the interests of eighteen per cent of the
Cypriot population were given precedence over those of the
majority (though neither faction was actually subjected to the

bother of being asked its opinion). The Greek government duly took up its exile in Egypt, while the British did have the grace to lift the ban on the Greek flag in Cyprus. In fact, they issued recruiting posters coloured in the Hellenic blue and white, urging young Cypriots to volunteer and 'Fight for Greece and Freedom'. Many thousands did so, forming a Cyprus Regiment in the British army. But the volunteers did not forget that Sir Michael Palairet had, only two years before, been instructed to discourage their enlistment in the army of Greece.

August 1945 was the last occasion on which the *enosis* card was played in purely British circles. The Greek Regent, Archbishop Damaskinos, was to pay a visit to London in September with his private secretary, the poet George Seferis. Sir Reginald Leeper, the British ambassador in Athens, devised a plan for making the visit coincide with an announcement of *enosis*. He was assisted in this by Philip Noel-Baker and by C.M. Woodhouse, the distinguished British Conservative politician and historian who had acted as liaison officer with the wartime Greek resistance. In a private but not confidential letter to me, C.M. Woodhouse describes how the project was defeated: '[Foreign Secretary Ernest] Bevin and the Foreign Office were favourably disposed, but the Colonial Office and the Chiefs of Staff strongly objected. I need not list their reasons, which are obvious. Bevin had been in office only for a few weeks, and he did not feel confident enough to force it through the cabinet. So that was that.'

Thus Britain missed the chance to requite Greece for its extraordinary wartime valour. The chance to meet Cypriot demands for self-determination at the same time was, obviously, missed as well. From then on, Cyprus was ruled to be a matter in which Greece had no right even to be consulted. In late 1953, after Greece had begun to recover from the racking civil war, Field Marshal Papagos, the Prime Minister, met Sir Anthony Eden, then Foreign Secretary, and again raised the question. Eden refused even to discuss it. The Greek Foreign Minister, Stephan Stephanopoulos, told Robert Stephens of the *Observer* that, 'Papagos came back and said to me in an outraged voice: "He told me *never* – not even *we shall see!*"' Greece resolved to raise the matter at the United Nations, but by that time the Greek Cypriots had decided to take a hand in making their own future. Preparations were already being made for a guerrilla war of liberation, which was launched with a fusillade of bomb explosions all over Cyprus on 1 April 1955. The explosions were the work of *Ethniki Organosis Kypriou Agoniston*: the National Organization of Cypriot Fighters, who became famous under the acronym of EOKA. With that fusillade, some would say that the modern history of Cyprus had begun.

None of this is to argue that *enosis* is today a good solution for Cyprus, or even that it would have been the best (or only) solution in the past. That is still a matter of heated dispute among the Greek Cypriots, as it was in April 1955. The leader of the *enosis* campaign that year was the notorious Colonel, later General George Grivas, who features a good deal in this chronicle. He and his policy were opposed by the Communist leadership on the island – which made Cyprus unique in fighting an anti-colonial battle in part *against* the Communist Party. Later, Cypriot Marxists were to debate, and some of them were to regret, that decision.

The official position of the Republic of Cyprus today is that *enosis* is neither feasible nor desirable. None the less, the Greek heritage of the island is undeniable. And it is important to realize that, historically, *enosis* was not the romantic and irrational idea it has so often been made out to be. As a national aspiration, however simplistic, it conformed perfectly well with the emergence of modern Greece and with the desire of Greek Cypriots, who were a small force in themselves, to have an ally in their attempt to escape from the British Empire. It may have been unrealistic, and its exponents were often fanatics and chauvinists. In the end, a foolhardy pursuit of *enosis*, encouraged by forces outside Cyprus who had quite other plans for the island and its people, brought about the catastrophe of 1974.

Enosis had many ambiguities and ironies. The greatest one was the reaction it created among the Cypriot Turks, and the opportunity it gave to that other great factor in the Cyprus equation – Turkey itself.

Cyprus and *Taksim*

There are two decisive facts about the eighteen per cent of Cypriots who are not Greek. The first is that they are a minority. The second is that they are Turkish. This statement of the obvious may be more illuminating than it seems at first glance. As a minority with a different language, religion and tradition, Turkish Cypriots should obviously command the sympathy bestowed on any comparable group. A country can often be judged by how it treats its minority citizens and many modern and 'advanced' societies fail to pass this elementary test with any credit. The experience of European Fascism has imbued civilized people with a special sensitivity to the position of racial and national minorities, and a special horror at their persecution or subjugation. There is no reason why the government of the Republic of Cyprus should be exempt from this standard, and the Turkish Cypriot leadership has always sought strenuously to portray Archbishop Makarios and his supporters and successors as bent on the liquidation of their people. The behaviour of General Grivas and Nicos Sampson, the two best-known Greek Cypriot ultra-Rightists, has made this claim both more and less credible. Archbishop Makarios himself told Orianna Fallaci in an interview in 1976 that he had been visited, during the 1964 intercommunal fighting, by Brigadier Dimitrios Ioannides, accompanied by Nicos Sampson, who had been a leading member of EOKA.

> He wanted to 'see me secretly to suggest to me a project that would have settled forever the problem of Cyprus'. He entered, he kissed my hand very respectfully, then, 'Your Beatitude, here is my project. To attack the Turkish Cypriots suddenly, everywhere on the island, and eliminate them to the last one.' I was astonished, speechless. Then I told him that I could not agree with him; I told him that I couldn't even conceive of killing so many innocents. He [Ioannides] kissed my hand again and went away very angry.

Nine years later, Dr Henry Kissinger would recognize Ioannides as the ruler of Greece. And, eight months after that, while making noises about the need to improve the position of the Turkish Cypriots, Kissinger would be the only outside leader to flirt with the idea of recognizing Nicos Sampson as President of Cyprus. But that is not the point here. Archbishop Makarios, who confirmed the story to me in an interview in 1977, was saying in effect that, if you remember what these two men did to their fellow-Greeks, their attitude to the Turks can be imagined.

All this needs to be said. I have visited the mass graves of Alloa and Maratha and Sandallaris, three little villages just outside the city of Famagusta, where hundreds of Turkish Cypriot civilian corpses were dug up like refuse in the ghastly summer of 1974. And I have toured the burned-out ruin of Omorphita, a Turkish Cypriot suburb that was devastated by Nicos Sampson's gang of terrorists in 1963. I have no difficulty in sympathizing with Turkish Cypriot fears, and I do not believe that they have been manufactured out of thin air.

So, why is it relevant that this minority is Turkish? It is relevant because Cyprus used to be ruled by Turkey, because Turkey never abandoned its claim on Cyprus as a possession, because Cyprus is only forty miles from Turkey and because the Turkish leadership, in Cyprus and in Ankara, has always opposed majority rule in the island. It is relevant because, until 1960, it was the Greek Cypriots who were the oppressed minority; disenfranchised and coerced by the vastly superior powers of Britain and Turkey combined. In the geographical setting of the eastern Mediterranean, the Greek Cypriots remain a tiny minority when compared to their Anatolian neighbour, and the Turkish Cypriots appear as a geographically separated section of a majority group. It is this 'double minority' aspect of the problem which, as in the cases of Northern Ireland and Palestine, makes Cyprus such a thorny and difficult case. When both sides feel themselves to be isolated and outnumbered in the face of the other, it is not difficult for racialists and irredentists to gain influence among them.

The Turkish Cypriots may have presented themselves to the outside world as another case of an endangered minority. But in Cypriot politics they have always been admirably candid. Here, for example, is the editorial written by their leader, Dr Fazil Kuchuk, in his newspaper *Halkin Sesi* (*Voice of the People*) on 17 August 1954 – before the Greek Cypriot revolt against Britain had even begun:

> Cyprus, let it be remembered, was, until 1878, a part of the Turkish Empire. In 1878 the island was ceded to Great Britain as a security against Russian threat. Great Britain took over Cyprus on the undertaking that she would hand her back to Turkey as soon as this threat was abated or receded. From 1878 until 1914 Great Britain ruled the island on trust for Turkey, but when in 1914 Turkey joined forces with the Axis, Cyprus was annexed to the British Empire.
>
> There is no need to look into the legality or the legal effects of this annexation. Let us grant that it was legal and correct from all points of view. Nevertheless, having regard to the close association of the two countries (Britain–Turkey), the ever-increasing Soviet threat to humanity and world security and the moral side of the question, it should be abundantly clear to all intelligent men that Great Britain cannot consider the handing over of the government to any nation except with the full consent and approval of its former owner – Turkey. Turkey was the undisputed owner of this 'house' just before Great Britain took it over on trust. If world events have ended that 'trust' during 1914–18, subsequent world events have certainly revived it from all moral points of view. The position of world affairs today as far as they concern Great Britain and Turkey are the same as they were in 1878. There is the Russian pressure on Turkey coupled with the bonds of friendship and alliance between Turkey and Britain. The cause of ceding Cyprus to Britain is still continuing; the time to consider handing back Cyprus to its former owner therefore may not have arrived. *But* if Great Britain is going to consider this *enosis* question at all or is going to quit the island she has a legal as well as a moral duty to call Turkey and hand Cyprus back to Turkey, and ask the Turkish government to deal with the *enosis* problem which the tolerant and ill-advised British administration has fostered in the island. From a legal as well as moral point of

view, Turkey, as the initial owner of the island just before
the British occupation, has a first option to Cyprus. The
matter does not end there. From a worldwide political point
of view as well as from geographical and strategical points of
view Cyprus must be handed to Turkey if Great Britain is
going to quit.

   This has been the attitude of the Turkish government.
They have never taken the Greek campaign for *enosis*
seriously because they believed that Great Britain's decision
not to quit the island was an unassailable answer to the whole
question; but they have made it emphatically clear that if
Great Britain ever considers leaving Cyprus then the Turkish
government has a great interest in the ownership of the
island. The Turkish youth in Turkey, in fact, has grown up
with the idea that as soon as Great Britain leaves the island
the island will automatically be taken over by the Turks. It
must be clear to all concerned that Turkey cannot tolerate
seeing one of her former islands, lying as it does only forty
miles from her shores, handed over to a weak neighbour
thousands [*sic*] of miles away, which is politically as well as
financially on the verge of bankruptcy.

Dr Kuchuk later became the first Vice President of the
Republic of Cyprus, but there is no reason to think that he ever
altered his opinion since he took the same line, in conversation,
until his death in January 1984. His 1954 editorial contains all
the essentials of the Turkish position – a colonial attitude to the
Greeks and a purely strategic attitude to the island. A few days
after he penned the lines quoted above, Kuchuk sent a telegram
to the UN Secretary General, Dag Hammarskjöld, saying that
his community, 'vehemently reject *enosis*, self-government or a
plebiscite'. This fairly exhaustive repudiation was music to the
ears of the British colonial authorities, who took the same line.
The Greek Cypriot majority were left with no alternative to the
status quo except revolt. So, while every other country in the
region – Egypt, Lebanon, Syria – was experiencing the pangs of
anti- or post-colonialism, Turkey and the Turkish Cypriot
leadership alone supported the status quo. Turkey did so by
joining the doomed Baghdad Pact; its proxies in Cyprus by

stepping forward to assist a British occupation that, after the Suez disaster of 1956, became obsolete as well as unjustifiable. Rauf Denktash, who was to succeed Dr Kuchuk as Turkish Cypriot leader, and who now heads the Turkish protectorate in northern Cyprus, conceded in his book *Five Minutes to Midnight* that he and his associates had 'supported colonial rule because we were unaware of changing world conditions'. But, even if Mr Denktash meant to profit from his mistake by admitting this, the damage had already been done.

Turkey as a country remained quiet about Cyprus after being on the losing side in the First World War. Kemal Ataturk was able to be generous towards Greece after inflicting such condign punishment on it in Asia Minor in 1922. For a brief period, he and Eleftherios Venizelos almost agreed to drop rival nationalist claims. But, in retrospect, Turkey's attitude to Cyprus seems to have been one of a resentment awaiting an opportunity. The resentment was supplied by the British, who under Disraeli had cheated the Sultan out of the island in the first place. The opportunity was also supplied by the British, who found that they needed Turkish intervention as a counter-weight to Greek demands some eighty years later.

It is an article of faith among Greek Cypriots that the British used 'divide-and-rule' tactics and were careless of their long-term communal effects. This widely held view, for which there was a good deal of evidence in any case, received an important confirmation as recently as 1982. C.M. Woodhouse wrote in his memoirs *Something Ventured* about the political situation on the island in 1954. It should be borne in mind that Woodhouse was an active and successful intelligence agent in the 1950s, and a man well connected in the British Conservative aristocracy. Doing down his own side would not come naturally to him. He wrote:

Harold Macmillan [then Foreign Secretary] was urging us to stir up the Turks in order to neutralize the Greek agitation. I wrote a minute in opposition to this tactic. I also asked the Prime Minister's private secretary if I could see Churchill on the subject, but he absolutely refused even to pass on the suggestion, which he clearly regarded as impertinent. I did not think it right to make use of the family connection to see him privately.

In a letter to me dated 10 September 1983, Woodhouse wrote:

> The minute of mine to which you refer was simply a manuscript note appended, with others, to the text of Macmillan's paper. It would therefore only be publicly available if and when Macmillan's own paper becomes available, which would not be until next year or the year after under the thirty-year rule. But even then departments have, as you know, the right to withhold particularly sensitive papers from the open files in the Public Record Office, and in this case I imagine they would do so.

In an interview with the Turkish daily paper *Tercuman*, published on 30 July 1983, former Turkish Foreign Minister Melih Esenbel recalled the same period and confirmed that his government saw the British strategy as one leading to *taksim* – the Turkish word for partition. He said that after Harold Macmillan became Prime Minister in 1956 he held secret talks with his Turkish counterpart Adnan Menderes. The subject of the talks was a ploy, made by the British Colonial Secretary, Alan Lennox-Boyd, to invoke partition as a foil against *enosis*. Esenbel told his interviewer:

> These secret talks were put in minutes. During these talks Macmillan gave some kind of assurance to our Prime Minister. According to this, the period of autonomy was reduced to seven years and the Turkish and Greek Cypriot representatives were to be on the Governor's administration. But to placate Greece they were given 'advisory' duty. Before, it was described as 'co-operation'. And when Macmillan also gave his assurance that after these seven years the right of self-determination will be used within the framework of Lennox-Boyd's statement and thus the road to *taksim* too would be opened, we assumed a positive stance.

As in the case of the Suez invasion, Britain was posing as the mediator between two warring parties in order to advance the cause of one of them. As in the case of Suez, it takes time for these things to come out.

It has often been debated whether Britain 'stirred up the Turks' or whether the Turks would, in any case, have mobilized themselves against Greek Cypriot nationalism. The distinction blurs under examination. What can be shown is that Britain, which refused to discuss the future of Cyprus with Greece because it was a strictly 'internal matter', consciously and without any such scruples drew mainland Turkey into Cypriot affairs. She also made every effort, as she had done in India and Palestine, to employ intercommunal differences as a means of control. Turkey's hesitation and isolation, the products of two unsatisfactory world-war performances, were definitively over-come by this seduction. It will, I hope, not be thought too schematic to list some examples which illustrate what Harold Macmillan meant by his sordid but clever stratagem.

1. In 1955, Dr Fazil Kuchuk was allowed to organize, with the declared help of a Turkish national named Hikmet Bil, a political party with the striking name of the 'Cyprus is Turkish Party'. This was at a time when all Greek parties were banned, and Britain claimed exclusive sovereignty over the island.

2. Later in the same year, at the London conference on Cyprus sponsored by Harold Macmillan, Fatin Zorlu, the Turkish Foreign Minister, insisted that if the British left the island should revert to Turkey. In his memoir, *Full Circle*, Sir Anthony Eden wrote of this demand that, 'It was as well, as I wrote in a telegram at the time, that they [the Turks] should speak out.'

3. At the same conference, Harold Macmillan publicly assured Zorlu that, 'We do not accept the principle of self-determination as one of universal application.'

4. In September 1955, at the close of the London conference, there occurred a tremendous anti-Greek pogrom in the Turkish cities of Istanbul and Izmir. The riots 'followed' a dynamite explosion in the Turkish consulate at Salonika, but erupted almost at the exact moment it took place. There was a definite pattern of organization to the riots, noticed at the time by prominent British conservative journalists such as Noel Barber

of the *Daily Mail*. Armenians and Jews were attacked as well as Greeks, and some $300 million-worth of damage done. The Greek presence in Istanbul has never been restored. At their trial in Ankara in 1960, the then Prime Minister Adnan Menderes and his Foreign Secretary Fatin Zorlu were accused and convicted of having fomented the riots in order to impress the British government with Turkish intransigence. No official British comment on the events was made at the time, though Greek Cypriots noticed that their demonstrations were put down with British armed force whether they were peaceful or not.

5. Though the Turkish Cypriot terrorist group Volkan was founded in 1955, and carried out many lethal attacks on civilians, very few members of it were ever tried, let alone punished by the British crown. In contrast, numerous sup- porters of the Greek Cypriot EOKA were hanged and hundreds more imprisoned. The British trained an exclusively Turkish mobile reserve to combat EOKA and employed many more Turks in the police and auxiliary forces. Members of these echelons were involved with Volkan, which later changed its name to the Turkish Defence Force or TMT*. In a celebrated case in 1958, a Turk, Sergeant Tuna, was convicted of possessing bombs and ammunition by a British court. The good sergeant, unlike his Greek counterparts, was allowed bail in his own recognizance and left immediately for Turkey.

6. In 1956 Alan Lennox-Boyd told the House of Commons that a Greek Cypriot demand for union with Greece would be met by a British-sponsored plebiscite for Turks only. If the Turkish Cypriots voted to join Turkey, the island would be partitioned. Thus, by demanding the whole of Cyprus, the Turks could be assured of getting at least half of it. Whereupon Dr Kuchuk demanded that the island be divided along the 35th parallel. The British interest in helping to stimulate this demand is too obvious to need underlining.

'Divide and Rule', of course, has come to translate histori- cally as 'Divide and Quit'. The British say that leaving (or partition) is the last thing they will do – and then it is the last

---

*Turk Mudafa Teskilat.

thing they do. Subsequent quarrels among the inhabitants can be taken as evidence that they just do not get on without British guidance.

Imperial favouritism towards the Turks did not 'work', in the sense that it did not succeed in crushing the Greek Cypriot rebellion. Nor did any policy succeed in this impossible objective. But it did succeed in damaging intercommunal relations very severely and perhaps permanently. It is important to remember that before 1955 there was no history of internal viciousness in Cyprus. The island had been aptly described as 'an ethnographical fruit cake in which the Greek and Turkish currants were mixed up in every town and village and almost in every street'. In spite of *political* clashes over the future of Cyprus, the Cypriots never had to endure the bitter, venomous, protracted hostility that was the experience of religious and national struggle in Crete and other islands warring on the Ottomans. Even during the First World War, with Britain and Greece on one side and Turkey on the other, there was no analogous hostility between Greek and Turkish Cypriots. It was only when Turks put on British uniforms to oppose a popular movement that they were shot at by Greeks. And even after that, it took some time before people resorted to the final obscenity of killing people just because they were Greek or Turkish. In his book *Years of Upheaval*, which attempts to postpone discussion of his own role in the Cyprus catastrophe to a later volume, Dr Henry Kissinger gives a misleading and self-serving account of the historical background. He speaks of 'primeval hatred of Greeks and Turks', 'atavistic bitternesses' and 'a lethal cocktail' (see pages 147–51). In doing so, he perpetuates a fairly widespread and commonplace view of the island's troubles; a fatalistic view of the incompatibility of the communities that insults both of them.

Sir Hugh Foot, now Lord Caradon, the last British Governor of the island and the one least inclined to play the bully or the manipulator, still gives the game away in some respects in his memoirs. In discussing the 1958 plan for limited self-government, which represented a retreat from the earlier policy of British *cum* Turkish colonial rule, he writes, in *A Start in Freedom*:

I knew of course that the Turks, *who were to be approached first*, would strongly dislike some aspects of the policy, and I wrote to the Deputy Governor on 7 January from London to say that everything would depend on whether the British government would stand up to the Turks. But I thought that our absolute assurance that no final decision on the future of the island would be made without Turkish approval might outweigh their objections. *They were in fact being given an absolute veto on long-term policy.* [italics mine]

Having thus confirmed Melih Esenbel's account above, Sir Hugh adds, with the sort of British fair-mindedness that tends to drive one wild: 'Much more difficult to persuade Archbishop Makarios and the Greeks, it seemed to me. But the return of the Archbishop to Cyprus, the ending of the Emergency, the promise of self-government might be sufficient to sway them.'

Archbishop Makarios, who had emerged as the spiritual and temporal leader of the Greek Cypriots, was then in Athens, having been deported and held without trial in the Seychelles islands before his release. In other words, if the Greek Cypriot majority would accept a Turkish 'absolute veto on long-term policy', they could be allowed the return of their chosen religious and political leader, the end of Emergency rule by foreign soldiers (though not the departure of those soldiers) and 'the promise of self-government' – which meanwhile looked rather qualified by the Turkish 'veto'. But Britain held the *force majeure*, and it was made clear to the Cypriots that they could choose only between this and a worse offer.

It took a while for the Turkish leadership to realize the bargain it was getting. Sir Hugh records the riots instigated from Ankara and the rough diplomacy exerted from the same quarter, noting that, 'Turkish intransigence was such that no conceivable proposal we put to them would be acceptable – short of partition.' But the British had failed to find any Greek Cypriot collaborators worthy of the name, and had been impressed by Aneurin Bevan's question in the House of Commons -- did they want a base *in* Cyprus or Cyprus *as a base*? Having opted for the former, and having lost their hegemony in Iraq, Jordan and Egypt, they were anxious to be off. The Turks were persuaded to settle on the basis of what became known as the London–Zurich agreements.

The 1960 Cyprus constitution (based on those agreements), and the associated Treaty of Guarantee, were unique in two major respects. The agreements were devised by three conservative governments in London, Athens and Ankara – none of them destined to last for very long. The Cypriots were simply presented with the results and told brusquely that if they did not accept they would be faced with partition. Actually, the constitution itself, whether by accident or design, contained the seeds of partition within it. It continued the old Ottoman and British colonial practice of creating separate categories of citizenship – now designated as Greek and Turkish instead of the traditional 'Muslim' and 'non-Muslim'. Separate municipalities were provided for. Greek and Turkish voters were to have separate elections. Civil service and police posts were to be shared in a ratio of seventy per cent Greek and thirty per cent Turkish; almost doubling the Turkish presence. In the army, in fact, the ratio was fixed at sixty–forty. The seventy–thirty ratio also obtained in the House of Representatives and the cabinet. The Vice Presidency of the Republic, reserved for a Turk, carried with it the right of veto. Turkey also won the right to station troops on the island, as did Greece. The Treaty of Guarantee gave the governments in Ankara, Athens and London the right to intervene in Cyprus either together or (in a clause inserted at the instigation of Turkey) alone. A 'separate majority' provision on matters concerning tax and electoral law gave the Turkish Cypriot minority an additional right of veto in the House of Representatives. In that House, separate majorities of Greek and Turkish members were required to modify fiscal, electoral or municipal laws. This meant that a bill supported by thirty-five Greek and seven Turkish members could in theory be defeated by eight Turkish votes. Those of us who today look kindly on measures of 'affirmative action' and 'positive discrimination' for minorities do so in order to compensate for past injustices. It is not obvious for which past discriminations the Turkish minority was being compensated.

Meanwhile, ninety-nine square miles of Cyprus were removed from the territory of the Republic and placed under

British authority. To this day, the Cypriot government has no jurisdiction over these bases or the uses to which they are put. No other democratic country has ever imposed or accepted conditions of that kind.

Cyprus, then, got a form of independence long overdue. But it was compelled to concede more than one-third of its legislative and administrative machinery, not to a minority, but to an eighteen per cent minority which, supported by a foreign country, had opposed that independence all along. It was an unpromising start. During the London negotiations, Archbishop Makarios raised thirteen objections to the agreements and presented them to the British Foreign Secretary, Selwyn Lloyd. Makarios was told to 'take it or leave it', with the clear implication that 'leaving it' meant partition and his own destruction. He took it.

Many, if not most, commentators on the unhappy years that lay ahead have stressed Greek and Turkish atavism, sectarianism, intransigence and intolerance. The word 'Byzantine' gets hurled around a good deal. Such observations fail to account for two things. One is that, even at the hour of their independence, the Cypriots were treated as objects rather than subjects in their own country and their own deliberations. The second is that a legacy of intercommunal tension and distrust had been created by outside powers, and then built into an imposed constitution. Most culpable in this were the British, whose crass and occasionally capricious policy had led to the bloodshed and discord in the first place. There are enough villains in the story without inventing new ones; this was not an occasion when Anglo-Saxon phlegm and fair-mindedness were seen to their best advantage.

Cyprus got its independence unnecessarily late, and under very trying and onerous conditions. Archbishop Makarios was right when he said that the agreement had created a state but not a nation. The fragility of its institutions and its alliances, internal and external, might have been overcome with time. But time, for various reasons, was something that Cyprus was not to be allowed.

II The Axe and the Woods

> When the axe came into the woods, the trees said, 'The
> handle is one of us.'
>
> Turkish proverb

The Cyprus problem involves questions of nationality, of
intercommunal relations, of strategy and of geopolitics. There
are, on the island, utterly conflicting interpretations of nation-
hood, independence and freedom. The Cold War is fought
quite energetically in Cyprus, which has three NATO armies on
its soil (one of them regarded by the majority of the population
as an aggressor rather than as a defender) as well as the world's
largest percentage of Communist voters (thirty-three per cent
of the Greek Cypriots regularly cast their ballots for AKEL, the
pro-Moscow party). And the geographic location of the island,
anchored so near the shores of Syria, Israel, Egypt and
Lebanon, has placed it in regional contention as well.

Definitions, like simplifications, are dangerous but necessary. In the post-1960 period the Cyprus problem can be
defined as the exploitation by outside powers of intercommunal
differences that were genuine in themselves. The purpose of the
exploitation was to suborn the independence of the island. This
theory has its difficulties, but it can be demonstrated as superior
to the vastly more simplistic model of 'Greek versus Turk'.

Of course, most of the local combatants engaged in the
struggles of the 1960s imagined themselves to be fighting for
their respective motherlands and heroic traditions. The urgency
of the battle against British rule had put the Greek Cypriots in a
position where the Orthodox Church, the Greek flag and the
intoxicating slogans of Hellenism had shaped their liberation.

And had they not defeated both the British *and* the Turks? From the start, a strong element of vainglory was present; the boastful conviction that *enosis* (explicitly ruled out, along with *taksim* by the 1960 agreements) was still attainable. Two prominent spokesmen for this view were Polycarpos Georgadjis, Makarios's Minister of the Interior, and Nicos Sampson, the publisher of the sensational newspaper *Makhi* (*Combat*). Both men had been prisoners of the British, and senior members of EOKA. Both were staunch chauvinists, who regarded the Cypriot Left as treasonous for its tepidity about the armed struggle and its relative internationalism. Both were unscrupulous and conspiratorial, strongly marked by mythic ideas about violence and gunplay. For them, and for a number of others, the EOKA struggle was unfinished and the EOKA ranks were not disbanded.

On the Turkish side, also, there was much undigested political and national resentment. The leadership regarded the 1960 agreements as at best a draw. The guerrillas of TMT kept their weapons and maintained their discipline. They detested the idea of Greek majority rule, which amounted in their eyes to rule by former subjects, and they found the idea of an Archbishop as President especially uncongenial. On the political level, Vice President Kuchuk and his associates were determined to interpret their large share of constitutional power very strictly and literally. They could do this in the confidence that Turkey was ready to support them and lay only a few miles away.

Nationalism is often strongest at its periphery. History has shown that Corsicans can feel more passionately French than Parisians, that Austrians can be more German than Berliners, that inhabitants of Ulster and the Falklands are more ostentatious with the Union Jack than are Londoners. In the modern history of Greece and Turkey, two of the most extreme nationalist politicians have been Cypriots. General George Grivas, born in Trikomo, made various unsuccessful and unpleasant forays into mainland extremist politics (leading a campaign of atrocity during the Greek civil war) before returning to Cyprus to command EOKA in 1955. He ended his days as the abject instrument of a Greek military junta whose true objectives, if we are to be charitable, may have been obscure to him. Colonel Alparslan Turkes, founder and leader of the Turkish National Action Party, was born in the village of Lefka and got into trouble during the Second World War for his pro-Nazi activities. He still nurtures the dream of a Greater Turkey, to be carved largely out of the Soviet Union (and China!) and in the 1970s his party's 'Grey Wolf' youth commandos were held responsible for thousands of murders and bombings in Turkey itself. He, too, helped bring a military dictatorship to power and found that its objectives were more cynical than his own. He, too, pressed for Cyprus to become the exclusive property of his own 'motherland', and he kept close links with TMT.

In the figures of these two febrile and narrow-minded men, one can discern the fanatical and violent mentalities which, apparently diametrically opposed to one another, have actually colluded in maiming Cyprus and in destabilizing democratic life and institutions in Greece and Turkey. These politicians and their followers would have been damaging enough in any situation which involved or demanded intercommunal tolerance. But, as well as acting as destroyers of Graeco–Turkish harmony they also lent themselves, as proxies, to external forces which sought the subversion of Cypriot independence.

All this, to the zealots of the 1960s, lay in the future. But the prostitution of nationalism was to start early on both sides. It was also to take valuable lives from the respective communities which it purported to defend – 'the axe in the woods'. Even before the British withdrawal, EOKA had turned its guns on democrats and Leftists who opposed its tactics and its xenophobia. In like manner, TMT slew numerous Turkish Cypriots who favoured Graeco–Turkish co-operation. An especial target in both cases was the Pan-Cyprian Workers Federation (PEO), an island-wide trade-union movement which, then as now, was intimately connected with the Communist Party. To the credit of PEO, whatever may be its political rigidity, it has always striven for a non-sectarian policy. Andreas Ziartides, its Secretary General, was the target of several EOKA *attentats*. Ahmet Sadi, director of its Turkish office, was forced to leave the island in 1958 after an assassination attempt by TMT.

Others, like Fazil Onder, Ahmet Yahya and Ahmet Ibrahim, were not so fortunate.

After 1960, as both sides circled around each other like scorpions in a bottle, it became even more imperative for the sectarian terrorists to crush independent or internationalist feeling. In the early years at least, Greek Cypriot Fascists did not shoot Greeks (they were to make up for this later). An atmosphere of euphoria, reinforced by a little moral blackmail, was enough to convince most Greeks that unity was paramount after the qualified triumph over Britain. On the Turkish side, however, life was extremely tense. On the very eve of independence, the British minesweeper HMS *Burmaston* had surprised the Turkish ship *Deniz* as it prepared to unload a cargo of illegal weapons in northern Cyprus. Other Turkish craft had been detained in suspicious circumstances, but the *Deniz* case is important because the vessel was caught before it could throw its contraband overboard, and because the incident shows how sincere were at least some Turkish elements about the new 'partnership state'. It also had the deplorable effect of convincing the EOKA veterans that they were right to prepare for a 'second round' with the Turks. Which, in turn, made the Turks nervous and intolerant.

Perhaps the worst and most portentous atrocity of this period was committed in April 1962, when two Turkish Cypriot editors raised their voices publicly against TMT and its separatist plans. Ayhan Hikmet and Ahmet Gurkan were the publishers of the weekly *Cumhurriyet* (*Republic*). They printed consistent criticism of the extremist Turkish leadership and even went so far as to threaten the publication of details about those who were planning racialist incitement and violence. Both Hikmet and Gurkan were murdered on 23 April, just before the edition in question could go to press. Emin Dirvana, the Turkish ambassador to Nicosia who had grown to dislike the Denktash faction and who later criticized it in print, denounced the murderers and, on his own initiative, attended the funeral of the victims. He was shortly afterwards recalled to Ankara. None of this is to make light of the fear felt by many Turkish Cypriots when real intercommunal fighting broke out just before Christmas 1963. Eye-witness accounts of this period are scant and murky, partly because few of the participants in the violence have very much to boast about.

The prelude to the 1963–4 disturbances had been, in a sense, inscribed in the provisions of the 1960 constitution. As its critics had anticipated, that constitution proved inoperable and, since they had had such a minimal role in drafting it, few Cypriots felt it to be sacred. The Turkish Cypriots had carried their separatism (with the constraints on dissent noted above) to the furthest extent. They had insisted on the separate municipalities, on the quota system in the public service, and on vetoing financial and budgetary legislation. None the less, when President Makarios proposed his thirteen revisions of the constitution in 1963, it was the Turkish government in Ankara which rejected them before Vice President Kuchuk could respond. The thirteen points would have decided the allocation of jobs and the weight of parliamentary votes in stricter proportion to population. As compensation, Dr Kuchuk's Vice Presidential position would have been enhanced. But, in essence, the minority veto would have been broken – and the Turks were not willing to surrender that privilege.

During the civil violence that followed, four crucial things happened – things that go some way to explain the later disasters and miseries of Cyprus:

1. The Greek irregulars often failed to make any distinction between Turkish mainland soldiers (who were present in the fighting), Turkish Cypriot guerrillas and Turkish civilians. It is true that some detachments did not indulge in pogroms or reprisals against civilians. It is also true that some of the fiercest engagements took place in suburbs of Nicosia such as Omorphita, from which Greeks had been expelled by Turks during British rule. It remains the case that disgusting acts of arson, sadism and vengeance were committed, unpunished. Nicos Sampson's group was especially culpable. The hateful practice of hostage-taking made its appearance on both sides. Various excuses have been offered ('The Turks put guns in the mosques') but they are mostly spurious or shamefaced. The Turkish Cypriots were made to feel threatened as Turks.

2. The Turkish forces, both local and imported, attempted to establish permanent positions. These strongholds were not, as

might have been expected, mainly in areas where Turkish civilians lived. They were in positions, like those at the crusader castle of St Hilarion, which commanded crucial roads or communications (St Hilarion dominates the main road from Nicosia to the northern port of Kyrenia). A partially successful effort was made to establish a Turkish enclave on the northern coast around Mansoura and Kokkina. Here again, the concern was not so much with the Turkish Cypriot population, very thin in that part of Cyprus, as with the idea of opening a salient within easy reach of mainland Turkey. Later intercommunal fighting was to follow the same pattern, with Turkish arms securing critical positions within the legal territory of the republic, and Greek arms doing to Turkish civilians what they could not or dared not do to Turkish soldiers. In these rather squalid encounters, the outlines of the later partition began to be discernible.

3. Outside powers took the opportunity to intervene. Once granted, this opportunity soon became a habit. Turkish jets flew low over Nicosia on Christmas Day 1963 (and what sort of minority, inquired the Greek Cypriots, who had no air force, was that?) The Turkish army contingent engaged directly with Greek guerrillas near Ganili. Greek mainland contingents took their own part in the fighting elsewhere. British troops left their bases to take up position along a 'Green Line' in Nicosia. As usual, the justification for all outside interventions was 'keeping the peace'. But a precedent had been founded, which all of Cyprus was later to regret.

4. The British were finally and definitely replaced, as the main outside arbiter, by the United States. As George Ball, Under-secretary of State and President Johnson's mediator, put it: 'The British wanted above all to divest themselves of responsibility for Cyprus.' Henceforth, it was to be in Washington rather than London that the major external decisions were taken.

As 1964 wore on, those precedents were built upon. General Grivas returned to the island to help organize a National Guard. Turkish 'volunteers' were landed through the Kokkina enclave mentioned above. British troops were replaced by a mixed United Nations force, which helped to demarcate other

Turkish enclaves, dominated by TMT, inside the city of Nicosia and elsewhere. The Makarios government attempted to prevent strategic materials from reaching these enclaves: a policy which was often interpreted callously at lower levels and resulted in the denial of building materials and other essentials. The Turkish mainland government retaliated by taking the deplorable step of making its own Greek minority a hostage. The remaining Greek population of Istanbul, to the number of some 8,000, was expelled and its property confiscated. To its credit, the Greek government did not retaliate against the Turks of western Thrace. More fighting broke out in the summer as the Greek Cypriots attempted to close down the Turkish military enclave at Kokkina, and Turkish planes replied by showering neighbouring villages with high explosive and napalm. President Inonu of Turkey mobilized for a full-scale invasion.

On the wider international front, the picture also darkened appreciably. President Johnson, concerned about the ill effects of the crisis on the NATO alliance, despatched the former Secretary of State, Dean Acheson, to report on the island and its future. Mr Acheson came up with a plan quite quickly. Its essential points, which involved the dissolution of the Republic of Cyprus, have been the basis for American policy ever since, so they should be summarized briefly:

1. Most of Cyprus was to be united with Greece in a partial consummation of *enosis*.

2. An area of the northern coast was to be awarded to Turkey as a military base and a political canton. Other Turkish cantons were to be autonomous within the Greek area, including one in the capital of Nicosia.

3. The small Greek island of Kastellorizon, off the north coast, was to be ceded to Turkey.

American policy was guided here by two principles, both of which remained dominant even when the plan had been rejected. First was the fear, often expressed by the less polished elements in the Johnson administration, that Cyprus might become, 'the Cuba of the Mediterranean', with Makarios as its 'cassocked Castro'. Of course, Cyprus is an island and Makarios had a beard. In few other respects was the analogy a good one. But it was true that the island had a strong Communist implantation, and that its foreign policy conformed to the Non-Aligned Movement established at Bandung, Indonesia.

Acheson is unlikely to have been very much influenced, even so, by this kind of vulgar demonology. He had a more pressing reason for trying to bring the island within the orbit of NATO. It was, from his point of view, the most businesslike way of appeasing both Greece and Turkey. By giving them both a slice of Cyprus, a quarrel within NATO could be averted and the threat from radical elements in both countries could be contained. The pleasure of neutralizing Makarios and his radical supporters would be considerable but incidental. Not for the first or the only time, American foreign policy-makers cared more about the 'big picture' than the details. Not for the first or the only time, they regarded the actual inhabitants of the island as a distraction from other, more lofty, imperatives.

It was in 1964 that Greek extremism and Turkish intransigence began, semi-consciously, to act in concert and to be recognized by the United States for their ability to do so. Archbishop Makarios rejected the Acheson Plan, which neither Athens nor Ankara had yet done outright. In this, he was staunchly supported by a majority of Greek Cypriots. From this rejection may be dated the official American opinion that he was a dangerous nuisance. George Ball had undisclosed contacts with General Grivas, who agreed to support the ideas of modified *enosis*, the inclusion of Cyprus in NATO and the strategic sop to Turkey. Grivas's record of extreme anti-Communism, which dated back to his command of a Fascist group during the Greek civil war, may have facilitated this rapprochement. Let George Ball tell the story in his own words.

In his memoirs, *The Past Has Another Pattern*, he details his hatred, personal and political, for Archbishop Makarios. He also devotes several passages to a show of his own solicitude for the welfare of the Turkish Cypriots. Then, in describing his efforts to implement the Acheson Plan, Ball writes:

> Meanwhile, our intelligence had reported the growing antipathy between Makarios and General George Grivas, the famous leader of EOKA. Though Grivas was, of course, a passionate advocate of *enosis*, he might, I thought, be

easier to work with than Makarios, so we established an
underground contact with Socrates Iliades, who was Grivas's
lieutenant and director of the defense of Cyprus. Meanwhile,
Grivas returned to Cyprus with a plan for *enosis* that
provided protection for the Turkish Cypriots living on the
island and compensation for those wishing to leave. *The fact
that the Grivas Plan also called for the ouster of Makarios
enhanced its attractiveness.*

These schemes were all upset when Makarios encouraged
the Greek Cypriots to attack Turkish Cypriot villages. [italics
mine]

This is an extraordinary series of admissions for an American
statesman to make. He boasts of contacts with armed irregulars
operating against a sovereign state, and does not conceal that
his intention was the 'ouster' of a popularly chosen President.
He does this, moreover, in the name of protecting the Turkish
minority. Yet his favoured instrument was the man who, that
very year, was bombarding Turkish Cypriot villages. Mr Ball's
final sentence is simply an untruth; it was Grivas – not Makarios
– who ordered and launched the attacks – attacks which could
only defeat his own purposes as well as the purposes of Mr Ball.
Nevertheless, Grivas had to convince his followers that they
were fighting for 'Hellenism' instead of the backstairs deal that
was being readied.

The Turkish government, meanwhile, also pursued a policy
which was blinded by ideology and propaganda and which could
have been designed to bring about what it purported to avoid.
Having persecuted and expelled the Greeks of Istanbul, it
began to harass the Dodecanese and Aegean islands which lay
off its coast. There were threats of retaliatory annexation if
Greece 'went too far' in Cyprus. Mitylene airport was buzzed
regularly by Turkish military jets, and local Greek fishermen
found themselves the object of unwelcome attention from
Turkish patrol boats. The declared intent of this policy was to
force Athens to lean on Makarios; to press him to lower his
guard and to modify his independence. But Makarios was not,
as the Turks were officially committed to believing, a creature
of the Greek government. Still, he was within reach of Greek

pressure. When that pressure was finally exerted, it was not of the kind that the Turks would have publicly admitted to wanting.

In making known his criticism of the Acheson Plan, Andreas Papandreou (then a minister, later to become the first Socialist Prime Minister of Greece) was speaking only as an individual but influential member of his father's party – the Centre Union. But he made a prescient point. The plan, he said, could be imposed on Cyprus only 'by the force of Greek arms'. Greece was prepared to consider the plan officially, but public opinion and the parliament were sure to support Makarios if he held out for independence from NATO. It followed, then, that either the Acheson plan or Greek democracy had to be changed. I almost wrote that it followed 'as the night the day'. That, in fact, would be too precise as well as too familiar a reference to what actually did happen. At least in part because of the need to 'solve' the Cyprus problem – when the 'problem' was its independence – Greek democracy was extinguished for seven years. Only since the night of dictatorship (1967–74) was lifted has it become possible to discover what was arranged in the dark, and by whom.

III Dragon's Teeth: Cyprus and the Greek Junta

Something from Cyprus as I may divine . . . It is a
business of some heat
William Shakespeare, *Othello*

In 1964 George Papandreou was the Prime Minister of Greece. In June he paid a visit to President Lyndon Johnson in Washington, (where there was an abortive attempt at a summit meeting with Prime Minister Ismet Inonu of Turkey). The visit was not a success. The Acheson Plan for the partition of Cyprus was not acceptable to Greek opinion. Johnson did more than hint that NATO aid might be withdrawn from Greece if it persisted in its obduracy, and that the United States might not defend Greece from a Turkish incursion into the Aegean. The elder Papandreou countered that, 'in that case, Greece might have to rethink the advisability of belonging to NATO'. Johnson struck a fresh note when he riposted that, 'maybe Greece should rethink the value of a parliament which could not take the right decision'. This was an astonishing way for the President of the United States to address the Prime Minister of a sovereign allied nation. But it was to be surpassed by the outburst to which LBJ treated Alexander Matsas, the Greek ambassador, a short time afterwards. The ambassador had told the President that, 'No Greek government could accept such a plan.' Johnson retorted:

Fuck your parliament and your constitution. America is an elephant, Cyprus is a flea. Greece is a flea. If these two fellows continue itching the elephant, they may just get whacked by the elephant's trunk, whacked good. . . If your

Prime Minister gives me talk about democracy, parliament
and constitution, he, his parliament and his constitution may
not last very long.*

In order to rub in his point, and the contempt that lay behind it,
Johnson added, 'Don't forget to tell old Papa-what's-his-name
what I told you – you hear?'

In July 1965 King Constantine of Greece, backed by the
traditional Right in the army and in politics, perverted the
Greek constitution and dismissed George Papandreou as
Premier. It was, yet again, General George Grivas who
provided the pivot between these forces by his decisive position
in Cyprus. Grivas was hostile to Archbishop Makarios and, as
we have seen, very friendly with Washington. He was also much
more 'understanding' of the Turkish position than his ultra-
nationalist rhetoric would have suggested. When Andreas
Papandreou, in concert with Makarios, rejected the Acheson
Plan, Grivas retaliated swiftly. He circulated documents, later
established even before a military court as blatant forgeries,
which alleged that there was a revolutionary conspiracy within
the Greek army, owing its allegiance to Andreas Papandreou.
The reactionary Defence Minister Petros Garoufalias, who was
later to become an apologist for the *real* military conspiracy,
gave currency to the allegations, which became known, after
the name of the fictitious conspiracy, as the 'Aspida' affair. It
was for seeking the resignation of Garoufalias, and for seeking
to uncover his connection with Grivas in Cyprus, that the elder
Papandreou came into conflict with King Constantine and was
forced from office himself. As the younger Papandreou put it in
his book *Democracy at Gunpoint*, written in exile in 1971,
'Cyprus lies at the heart of the tragic political developments that
have led to the death of democracy in Greece.'

After the King's unconstitutional putsch, there followed an
undignified two years of caretaking and powerbroking, but it
proved impossible to sanctify a legitimate pseudo-conservative
government in office. But there was, in fact, a conspiracy being

* See Lawrence S. Wittner, *American Intervention in Greece*. Columbia
University Press, 1982.

prepared in the armed forces. I have interviewed General George Koumanakos, Greece's most decorated officer, and then of the Military Staff College, who told me how in 1965 he was approached by a senior official of the United States embassy (whose name he gave me). Koumanakos had been a commander of Greek forces in the Korean war, and had many American friends. He was known as a strong anti-Communist. What his visitor wanted to know was, 'George, why are you not coming in with us?' Koumanakos suspected that there was a group of officers preparing to take political power, but he did not realize until then why they seemed so sure of themselves.

New elections were called for 28 May 1967, and Papandreou *père et fils* campaigned strenuously for a new mandate. They promised to keep the King within constitutional limits, to put the army under genuine civilian control, and to reduce Greek dependence on the favour of the United States.

They openly challenged the unelected 'para-state' that had ruled Greece since the end of the civil war in 1949. The principal institutions of the 'para-state' were the Palace, the General Staff, elements of the Church hierarchy and the American embassy. Their ancillaries were the KYP (the Greek subsidiary of the CIA) and the Joint US Military Aid Group Greece (JUSMAGG). The 'para-state' had shown its power before, in the 1961 elections, characterized by extensive violence and fraud, which resulted in the return of Constantine Karamanlis and his centre-right National Radical Union (ERE). It had shown its fangs in the murder of the Socialist deputy Gregory Lambrakis in Salonika in 1963, and in the attempts to protect the culprits in that murder. Soon thereafter, even Karamanlis himself had felt the force of the 'para-state' when he tangled with the ex-Nazi Queen Frederika, whose relations with the American embassy and with extreme conservative politicians were famously intimate. (There had even been protests from staff at the embassy who had had to spend official time planning for her shopping needs.) In that confrontation, it was Karamanlis who had to abdicate.*

* In interviews with the Athens *Daily Post* in 1966, Senator Strom Thurmond of the Armed Services Committee, and Admiral Arleigh Burke of the Center for Strategic Studies, both called on Queen Frederika to intervene in the Greek

On 21 April 1967, the 'para-state' decided that it could no longer coexist with formal democracy, and decided to forestall a Papandreou election victory by seizing power. Historians and analysts have argued since about American complicity in the military coup, but they have argued only about the extent of it. Many authoritative writers assert that the United States was preparing to support a later, more 'respectable' coup, commanded by generals rather than by the undistinguished colonels who actually struck on 21 April. The evidence for this opinion is mainly negative – there was 'surprise' at senior levels of the State Department and the American embassy, and many senior intelligence operatives claimed to have been caught napping. Evidence for direct American complicity is also somewhat suggestive. Colonel George Papadopoulos, who led the coup, had been on the payroll of the CIA since 1952 and acted as the chief liaison officer between the Greek KYP and its senior partner in Langley, Virginia. Moreover, he had used a NATO contingency plan, designed to counter unrest in the event of a 'hot' war in the Balkans, to activate his putsch.

In his book, *Prescriptions for Prosperity* (1983), Lyndon Johnson's former friend and confidant Eliot Janeway describes a visit to Athens with Senator Vance Hartke in the autumn of 1966: 'To our surprise, our visit coincided with the preliminaries for the Greek military putsch, sponsored by the CIA and the DIA (the undercover Defense Intelligence Agency, an arm of the Department of Defense).' Janeway recounts Johnson's rage at his disclosure of this in a confidential bulletin. The elephant's trunk was getting ready to strike.

The dispute about the United States' complicity in the junta is, in any case, based on a false antithesis. The United States administration had sown the dragon's teeth that sprang up in the shape of the junta. The administration gave encouragement, training and materials to the anti-constitutional forces before the coup, and it became their patron and protector for seven years afterwards.

---

political crisis. Admiral Burke also said that he had heard of plans for a coup. The book that contained these interviews, by Elias P. Demetracopoulos, was banned by the junta as soon as it took power.

Cyprus, and the person of General Grivas, continued to form an important element in the junta's plan. Grivas had made it known publicly that he considered himself to be under orders from Athens while he commanded the Cyprus National Guard. He might bellow for *enosis* but he was working for partition all the same. The junta's own Cyprus strategy confirmed this rather tortuous analysis. It spoke continually of a cleansed and reborn country: 'a Greece for Christian Greeks'. It inveighed against all weakness and decadence, and it flirted with ideas of a greater (which is to say larger) Greece. But, like all similar Fascist systems, it was fundamentally unpatriotic, and engaged in furtive mortgaging of Greek interests to outsiders. The nationalist trumpetings were for mass consumption only – a task made easier by the forcible monopoly of Greek press and media which the junta now enjoyed.

Papadopoulos, the new strong man, went to a meeting with the Turkish mainland leadership on the border between the two countries at the Evros river. The meeting was intended to consummate a secret Paris meeting held between the Greek Admiral Toumbas and the Turkish minister Ihsan Caglayangil. It would have proclaimed *enosis* while conceding the basis for partition, and would have made the junta appear 'statesman-like'. This grandiose *démarche* got Papadopoulos nowhere. The Turks knew that extra Greek forces had been secretly placed on Cyprus under previous governments and demanded their withdrawal. Only with this proviso would the Turks agree to the Acheson proposal for a carve-up between the two countries. They sensed an advantage with the untried Greek government and were determined to press it home. Next month, in November 1967, General Grivas launched attacks on two Turkish Cypriot villages – Ayios Theodoros and Kophinou. The Turks once more threatened invasion, and the Greek government had to admit that it, rather than the Cypriot government, was responsible for Grivas's action. No better excuse could be found for the withdrawal of the 12,000 extra Greek troops from Cyprus, as well as of Grivas himself. With the good offices of Cyrus Vance, this was done. Henceforth, whether a Turkish invasion of the island took place on a good pretext or a bad one, it would be substantially unopposed. And the Turks had another justification for pointing to Greek perfidy.

Among the officers and men withdrawn to Greece that year were many democrats and patriots, who were gradually to be purged from the army altogether. Their replacements (because a small, legal Greek contingent still remained, as did a Turkish one) were to be hand-picked for their fanaticism and their indoctrination. The Acheson Plan, like many United States policies, might look superficially rational even if a bit crude, but those chosen to execute it were anything but rational.

While the balance was shifting against him in Athens and in other capitals, Archbishop Makarios had been consolidating his position in Cyprus. He had won almost unanimous political support from all the civilian parties. And two international developments had strengthened his position.

The first of these had come in 1965, with the report of the United Nations special mediator in Cyprus, Señor Galo Plaza of Ecuador. In his report to the UN Secretary-General, U Thant, Galo Plaza rejected the idea of partition and affirmed the right of the island to remain united and independent. He also opposed the physical separation of the two communities within the island, and strongly implied that the Turkish leadership was practising a form of self-segregation with partitionist objectives in mind. He called for a charter of rights for the Turkish Cypriots, to be supervised and enforced by the United Nations presence. And he called (rather more vaguely since he had no jurisdiction over the British bases) for the island to be 'demilitarized'. Most of this was at least acceptable to the majority of the Greek Cypriots (Andreas Papandreou in his *Democracy at Gunpoint* described Makarios as 'jubilant' about it, Robert Stephens in his *Cyprus: a Place of Arms*, as less than that). In any event, the Cyprus government officially welcomed the report.

Makarios thought that he had also kept the Turks at bay in the larger context. When President Ismet Inonu had threatened to invade Cyprus, he had been told to refrain in almost intolerably brusque terms by President Johnson. Johnson told Inonu that if he sent his invasion fleet to the island, the United

States would not feel obliged to guarantee his country against any Soviet response. Humiliated, Inonu climbed down. From this episode can be dated a Greek Cypriot superstition that somehow the United States would 'never allow' a Turkish invasion.

By 1968, it is probably fair to say that Makarios enjoyed general support in Cyprus for his policy of independence. True, most Greek Cypriots still felt Greek, and celebrated Greek national holidays with feeling as they had done for centuries past. But the economy was doing well out of independence, and a class of specifically Cypriot entrepreneurs was emerging. The reputation of Makarios abroad was high; higher than if he had been a prelate or regional chieftain in Greece itself. At home he was perhaps the only political leader in the world who could genuinely gain ninety per cent of the votes in an unfettered election.

Yet all of these gains were under threat. The Turkish government rejected the Galo Plaza report (again, Ankara announced its rejection before the Turkish Cypriots had said anything) and succeeded finally in securing Plaza's resignation. There were people in Makarios's own entourage, notably the Interior Minister, Polycarpos Georgadjis, who disliked the renunciation of *enosis* which acceptance of the report implied. In Athens the junta was crushing all opposition even from the feeble King Constantine. And, by the end of 1968, Richard Nixon had been elected President of the United States. The Nixon administration and the junta both detested Makarios, and both owed each other favours.

Students of the art of coup-making have had a great deal of field-research experience in the last decade or so. It is now quite well understood that those who wish to replace a popular government by force must proceed carefully. There must be pretexts, there must be uncertainty, there must be a good cause in which the deed is apparently done. Meanwhile there are newspapers to be 'influenced' and politicians to be 'brought over'. There are ugly elements – assassins, smugglers and the like – who are indispensable but who must be, in the argot of

the trade, 'deniable'. There are backers who must be protected;
their investment becomes worthless if it is disclosed.

In its campaign to remove Makarios and to achieve '*enosis* by
partition', the Greek junta had several major allies. It did not,
however, have them operating in harmony. It enjoyed a
monopoly of force in Greece, and a sizeable presence in
Cyprus. It had the Greek flag, with which to confuse simple-
minded patriots. It had the allegiance of disparate Cypriot
forces who felt that Makarios had reneged on *enosis*, but these
were volatile. It had the Turkish and Turkish Cypriot leadership, who officially detested all Greek aspirations but who
might hope for something if the seemingly impregnable
Makarios were removed. And it had the Americans, who
regarded Makarios as a pest, who had not forgiven him his
obduracy in 1964, and who had an interest in removing Cyprus
from the grasp of a professed 'neutralist'.*

Not all of these forces wanted the same thing for the same
reasons, and few of them could be seen to act at the behest of,
or even in concert with, western Europe's most brutal and
unpopular government. It was, all the same, a formidable list of
enemies for the agile Makarios to confront – whether separately, in sequence or all at once.

All of these enemies conducted their policy on two levels.
The Greek junta had to affect concern for the Greek Cypriots
and for 'Hellenism'. It maintained formally correct relations
with the Republic of Cyprus, though it suspected its government (correctly) of sheltering anti-junta Greeks from the
mainland. The Turkish government, which was undergoing
frequent changes and experiencing painful political upheavals
at home, and which was moving towards its own experience of

---

* Confirmation of this bizarre line-up may be found in *Stin Proti Grammi
Amynis* (*In the First Line of Defence*), a tremendously unattractive book written
by Constantine Panayotakos and published in Athens by Loukas Giovanis.
Panayotakos was the junta's ambassador in Cyprus (1971–72) and in Washington (1972–74). His book, which draws upon junta archives, denounces
Makarios for his hostility to *enosis*, his willingness to compromise with the
Turkish Cypriots and his flirtation with the Left. Above all, it excoriates his
opposition to any scheme of partition with Turkey that might have saved the
junta's fate.

military rule, continued with its long-established policy. That is to say, it presented itself internationally as the guarantor of a threatened minority. And it persisted with its long-term advocacy of partition. Under United Nations auspices, both sides on the island paid lip-service to the intercommunal talks; a long-running and patient but generally disappointing exercise conducted by Glafkos Clerides, a senior Greek Cypriot lawyer and parliamentarian, on the one side and Rauf Denktash, of whom more later, on the other. Both men were political conservatives, with British legal backgrounds. Beneath their *politesse* the basic differences lay unresolved. Progress on the intercommunal front was indeed being made, but it was made, as Galo Plaza had pointed out, because of the decency of the Cypriot people and their long, if not now unbroken, history of village-level friendship.

The United States administration also operated on what Washington jargon nowadays calls a 'two-track' system. Although it was not a formal or legal guarantor, America had extensive treaty commitments to Greece and Turkey, and maintained a large embassy in Cyprus. It was also using the British 'sovereign' bases, with the tacit approval of Makarios, to overfly the Middle East with U-2 and other aircraft. In theory, its official policy was that of a powerful mediator with friends in all camps. In fact, it was becoming increasingly committed to the Fascist-minded junta in Athens. Here, a peculiar symbiosis emerged. The junta needed, for its own reasons, to do something about Cyprus that would vindicate its claim to have renewed Greek life and Greek pride. And the United States needed to use Cyprus to fortify its position in both Ankara and Athens. In this imperfect relationship, both sides thought that they could exploit the other. It was an understanding that was to have dismal consequences, based as it was on American complicity with the dictators, and the cynicism of the dictators about American aid.

This had severe results for Greece, as is now universally acknowledged. But it had appalling consequences for Cyprus. Beginning in 1970, the Colonels began a sustained campaign against President Makarios. The campaign was supposed to employ violence only as a last resort, after measures of political isolation had been taken. But, the Greek junta being what it was, the campaign was crude and violent from the start.

The first instrument of the Colonels was Polycarpos Georg-adjis, the aforementioned Minister of the Interior. He had a record as an EOKA man, and also as a violent and conspiratorial individual. His position as minister, with its police links and secretive possibilities, had made him an over-mighty subject and had led Makarios to dismiss him in 1969. His willingness to accept outside commissions to 'deal with' local radicals, and his abuse of power, had made him intolerable as a member of an independent government. Out of office, Georgadjis agreed to work for Colonel Papapostolou, a Greek junta officer, in an early attempt to eliminate Makarios. In a conversation with his successor at the Interior Ministry, Mr Anastasiou, he boasted that, 'the Americans are behind us' and thus became the first of many naïve conspirators to believe that he enjoyed an actual guarantee of immunity – 'protection' – from the most powerful country in the world. The American embassy in Nicosia, which under its ambassador David Popper was officially concerned with maintaining cordial relations, either did not know or did not care about CIA connections with Papapostolou and Georgadjis. At any rate, it warned Makarios of something that only the CIA could have known – the existence of a junta-backed assassination plot. It is no disrespect to Ambassador Popper to say that his warning raised as many questions as it answered. His CIA chief of station, Eric Neff, had close contacts with Georgadjis and with other anti-Makarios and junta agents (a legacy of that 'underground contact' established by George Ball). Neff would regale diplomatic circles with his opinion, which was that Makarios was a menace and should 'go'. In the end it was Neff who went; recalled at the request of the Cyprus government. But before that, the friend and client of the loud American had made his move.

It was on 8 March 1970, almost a fortnight after Makarios received Popper's warning, that his helicopter was shot down as it lifted off from the roof of the Presidential Palace. Though the pilot was horribly injured by the shots, the President was able to walk unscathed from the wreck and to set a precedent for many future narrow escapes. Georgadjis was detained while trying to board a flight in some haste, but was not held on condition that he did not try to leave the island. Ten days after the assassination attempt, he went to a night-time rendezvous with Colonel Papapostolou and another Greek officer. The promise to get him out of Cyprus was not kept. Instead, he was shot through the head. The CIA station in Athens overruled all calls for an inquiry. It was the Greek junta which planned both the assassination and, according to eye-witnesses, the silencing of the assassin.

Frustrated in its effort to get its way by a single stroke of murder, the junta began a broader campaign of subversion. It helped General Grivas to return secretly to the island, in violation of the 1967 agreement with Turkey. Grivas set about building a long-term terrorist underground, which he christened EOKA-B. This time, its targets were to be Greek Cypriots, especially Makarios supporters and the Communist and Social-ist parties. At the more respectable level, but also with the connivance of Athens, a Co-ordination Committee for the Enosis Struggle (ESEA) was launched. It contained jurists and politicians, and was supported by newspapers receiving subven-tions from the junta.

While subversion and terror were being prepared under-ground, with Greek officers directly arming and training the members of EOKA-B and spreading its message among the young recruits of the National Guard, clumsy attempts were made to overthrow Makarios at the 'political' level as well. After their narrow escape from exposure in the Georgadjis affair, neither the junta nor its patrons wanted to resort to force if they could avoid it. But Makarios, at the political level, could always out-general them. He easily survived a farcical attempt at an 'ecclesiastical coup', when three obscurantist Cypriot bishops (of Kition, Kyrenia and Paphos) made the astonishing discovery that he should resign because he was violating Canon Law. The clerics, all of whom were *enosis* fanatics closely linked to the Athens dictatorship, affected the belief that religion and politics did not mix. This was more than hypocrisy on their part; it was in conflict with the Church's long role as spokesman for national aspirations. Makarios could not be beaten in his own synod, and it was the three bishops who ended up defrocked.

Defeated at the medieval, theological level, the junta switched to Cold War tactics in an effort to isolate and overthrow Makarios. In January and February 1972 it protested at his importing arms from Czechoslovakia to equip his police and security forces. Makarios was trying to build up a cadre that would be free of the taint of Athens and impervious to its infiltration. He was confronted by an arrogant letter from the Greek dictator George Papadopoulos, which demanded that he turn over the Czech weapons to the junta-officered National Guard, crack down on the Cypriot Left, and dismiss the Foreign Minister Spiros Kyprianou (now President of the Republic). Even as the letter was being delivered, junta and EOKA-B units were put on stand-by for a coup, in anticipation of Makarios's refusal of the *démarche*. Significantly, the Turkish government supported the Greek junta in this exertion of pressure. At a NATO meeting in Lisbon, there had been a confidential meeting between the Greek and Turkish foreign ministers, Panayiotis Pipinelis and Ihsan Caglayangil, where the Turkish minister had given the junta a deadline to come up with a 'final solution' to the Cyprus problem.

Again, Makarios managed to outwit his foes by an adroit mixture of concessions and defiance. Spiros Kyprianou resigned without waiting to be sacked, which took some wind out of the junta's sails. And the Cypriot police made surprise raids on EOKA-B hideouts (many Makarios loyalists were ex-members of the original EOKA, and knew the ropes). Unmistakable preparations for a coup were discovered, which Makarios boldly presented to the American embassy. Ambassador David Popper relayed the concern to Washington and to Athens, and Papadopoulos, caught off balance, was persuaded to stay his hand. But, in the course of his meeting with Makarios's envoys, Popper uttered a sentence which has never been forgotten by Cypriots. Confronted with the evidence of a coup to be mounted by a foreign government enjoying warm relations with the United States, he said, 'I am not authorized to tell you anything.' This raised the inescapable question: if the United States government could get a coup called off, could it not also authorize one?

The patience, if that is the word, of the Athens junta was

becoming exhausted. It wished, if at all possible, to present the coup as a rising by patriotic Cypriots against the 'Red Priest', whom it now referred to contemptuously by his baptismal name of 'Mouskos'. But, with declining support in Cyprus, it had to rely increasingly on its own strength, and that of its backers. In early 1972 Leslie Finer visited Cyprus. He is a commentator with a well-earned reputation for expertise in Greek affairs, and a no less well-earned reputation for political moderation. As the correspondent for the BBC in Athens, he had originated reports and broadcasts considered authoritative and prescient. His report on this occasion, 'The Colonels' Bid for Cyprus', appeared in the *New Statesman* of 10 March 1972, and deserves to be quoted at some length:

> It is impossible, unless you see it with your own eyes, to imagine the extent to which this secret army of junta officers have penetrated the fabric of public life in Cyprus. Lavishly paid, enjoying all kinds of tax and customs privileges . . . and handling large sums of money for oiling the machine and winning friends, these mercenaries have firmly planted the flag of the Colonels in Cyprus.

'For the Colonels,' wrote Finer, 'Grivas provides the ideal fuse to ignite a conflict which would enable the Athens regime to intervene to "restore order" and finally close their grip on the island.' He went on:

> Is Grivas, then, so unsophisticated that he is unaware of his passive role as a tool of Athens, believing that he is fighting for his beloved *enosis* cause, yet actually helping towards the hated solution of partition? It would seem impossible. Yet, having collaborated painfully with the man for months over the English edition of his memoirs, I can testify that he is quite capable of that degree of obtuseness.

George Ball had not then made public the secret agreement between Grivas and the CIA, so Mr Finer had to work from specialist knowledge and induction to write the following crucial sentences:

It is impossible to grasp what is happening in Cyprus now except on the basis that the Athens regime is paying for its keep by serving long-term American design: the removal of Makarios. . . It is, in other words, very far from a coincidence that the latest episode in the Cyprus crisis occurs simultaneously with the indecently hasty decision of President Nixon to override the Congress ban on arms shipments to Greece, and the continuing negotiations for a giant home base in the Piraeus for the United States' Sixth Fleet.

The American design was not, of course, limited to Cyprus. But during the two Nixon administrations, the Greek junta was more and more indulged by Washington. The Johnson administration had at least gone through the motions of disapproval, imposing a selective embargo on the shipment of arms and uttering occasional routine pieties about the eventual return of democracy.

On one famous occasion, Lyndon Johnson had even interceded to save Andreas Papandreou. In his memoirs, *A Life in Our Times*, Professor John Kenneth Galbraith tells how he approached LBJ on behalf of numerous American economists who had known Papandreou professionally while he was teaching in the United States. As Galbraith tells the story:

> In the early-morning hours my phone rang once again. It was Nicholas Katzenbach, then Under-secretary of State, calling to read with a greatly audible chuckle a message he had just received from the President: 'Call up Ken Galbraith and tell him that I've told those Greek bastards to lay off that son-of-a-bitch – whoever he is.'

To the last, Johnson persisted in pretending not to know (see page 62) how to pronounce a perfectly easy Greek name. And, *mutatis mutandis*, the same suspicion applies to him as later applied to ambassador David Popper and the Nixon administration. If he could stop 'those Greek bastards' he could also start them.

However close American–Greek relations were under

Johnson, with Nixon they became warm, rotten and corrupt. The extent of the intimacy between the junta and Washington has become better understood with the passage of time. It was only in 1983 that Seymour Hersh was able to reveal in his book *The Price of Power: Kissinger in the Nixon White House* that the junta had directly contributed money to the Nixon–Agnew election campaign in 1968. Nixon's ambassador to Athens, Henry Tasca, confirmed the transaction to a House of Representatives Intelligence Committee investigation (see pages 79–80 below). But this symbiotic relationship, involving arms sales, political favours and influence peddling, was possible only because of a pre-existing and durable 'understanding' between conservative military and political forces in both countries.

With Nixon, the practices of the junta, whether internal or external, were no further obstacle to American military aid. Vice President Agnew and Commerce Secretary Maurice Stans, among others, visited Athens and publicly praised the dictatorship. A senior American officer publicly compared the rule of the junta to the age of Pericles. Arms shipments, disguised as the sale of 'surplus' hardware, increased by $10 million each year until, on 22 September 1970, the embargo was formally lifted. National Security Decision Memorandum (NSDM) number 67, which found its way into Seymour Hersh's hands, explicitly stated that the Nixon administration would take, 'at face value and accept without reservation' any assurances about democratic reform that Papadopoulos cared to make. This consummated the advice given a year earlier by Nixon to Henry Tasca: 'We've got to restore military aid; as far as the rest is concerned, make it look as good as you can.'

The restoration of American arms sales was closely tied to another decision – the decision to 'home-port' the United States' Sixth Fleet in Greece. The home-porting plan was 'prematurely' disclosed, to the press and to Congress, on 21 January 1972. The Pentagon and the State Department both expressed extreme annoyance. But, by September 1972, all formalities had been completed, and United States destroyers were dropping anchor in Phaliron Bay, outside Athens. A carrier task force soon followed. The architect of the hom.-

porting agreement, Admiral Elmo Zumwalt, the Chief of Naval
Operations, had to overcome sustained objections from Greek
democrats and their supporters in Congress, led by Congressman Ben Rosenthal of New York. The administration attempted to evade the holding of hearings, but was outmanoeuvred
and had to put its case in public. The result was not edifying. In
an interview with Thomas Keagy and Yiannis Roubatis, authors
of the definitive study of home-porting, Admiral Zumwalt
made it clear that he 'viewed the presence of a military
government in Athens as an opportunity rather than a liability'.
He also professed to believe that the Greek junta's promises of
a move to democracy, at some future indefinite time, were
genuine. Rodger Davies of the State Department (who, as
ambassador to Cyprus, was later to be killed during the violence
created by the junta's 1974 coup) took the same line, naïve or
cynical according to taste. He told Congress that, 'a continuous,
quiet diplomatic dialogue between the government of Greece
and its allies is more conducive to the end [of restoring
democracy] than open criticism and challenge'. This early
exponent of 'quiet diplomacy' mistook, in his belief that 'the
only question is one of timing', the real relationship between
the two governments, and the real nature of the dictatorship.
By home-porting its fleet under junta auspices, the United
States became almost as dependent on the dictators as the
dictators already were on the United States. A vested American
interest in the survival of the junta had now been created. The
description of the state of affairs which now became current –
that the United States was 'in bed' with the Greek despots – was
crude but unhappily accurate.

As in many similar cases, American leniency with the regime
did not have the effect of mellowing, let alone of reforming it.
Quite the contrary. Secure in its role as little Greek brother, the
junta became markedly worse. In the summer of 1973, units of
the Greek navy mutinied against the junta. This revolt, which
challenged its claim to be a loyal and reliable defender of the
West, caused the dictatorship to lash out even at conservative
and monarchist officers whom it suspected of insufficient
enthusiasm.

In November 1973 the students of the Athens Polytechnic,

joined by numerous young members of the working class and the unemployed, rose against the Papadopoulos regime. Their protest was met with tanks and infantry and resulted in a heavy loss of life. But it put an end to a period of suspended animation in Greek politics. Exile and underground movements were galvanized. So was the hard core of the junta. Brigadier Dimitrios Ioannides, the head of the Greek Military Police (ESA) and a man long identified as the most ruthless member of the Papadopoulos junta, moved to replace his boss on 21 November. (It was Ioannides, it will be recalled, who had proposed the extermination of the Turkish Cypriots to Archbishop Makarios in 1964.) He could be reasonably certain that the American embassy, which occupied the building opposite his headquarters, would not object. For one thing, it had never protested about the torture which was known to go on in ESA's basements, and which had been verified by the Council of Europe. For another, the Americans had been disappointed by the failure of Papadopoulos, one month earlier, to allow United States aircraft to use Greek airspace to resupply Israel during the Yom Kippur war. For another, numerous members of the Papadopoulos entourage had become an embarrassment because of their corruption. The United States, as far as can be determined, did not involve itself in the fall of Papadopoulos. But nor did it try to keep him from being replaced. And it established a 'business-as-usual' relationship with his successor.

If Papadopoulos was a Fascist in the Mussolini mould, Ioannides was more like an authentic Nazi. He despised the laxness and corruption of his former associates; he was a sadist and a believer in extreme military cultism; he did not seek the love of his subjects as long as they feared him. He had been formed within a very narrow compass, knowing only Greece and Cyprus and those mainly through his experience in uniform. His genocidal proposal to Makarios was typical of him rather than exceptional. Having put Papadopoulos under house arrest and unleashed his secret police on all manifestations of dissent, Ioannides began to speed up the war on Makarios. Gone was the crafty policy of undermining Cyprus in unspoken concert with Turkey. The new dictator wanted ruthless, rapid results. And he still had the weapons bequeathed to him by his predecessors and by the Pentagon.

Conciliation was, for Ioannides, synonymous with cowardice. He now knew that Makarios was sheltering a number of anti-junta Greeks on Cyprus. He suspected Cypriot Leftists of involving themselves with the Polytechnic revolt. He had a bigoted antipathy to deals with Turkey, though some of his General Staff still felt that an agreement with Ankara was the only risk-free way to a version of *enosis*. One might say that Ioannides thought any *enosis* was better than none, and the United States thought that any partition was better than none. That belief in a workable coincidence of interests was to prove not just cynical but lethal. Within a year, it brought disaster to Cyprus and near-disaster to Greece and Turkey.

Kissinger

To concede to Henry Kissinger an omnipotence in decision-making during the year 1974 is tempting but misleading. For one thing, it is to take him at his own valuation, and the valuation of his many admirers. As is customary in the case of 'great statesmen', when things go well they claim full credit. And when things do not go well, ineluctable and uncontrolled forces can be blamed. So it was with Kissinger over Cyprus. The Secretary of State, who normally loved to pose in front of the press and the public as a man on top of his brief and at ease with international affairs, preferred in this case to claim that it was all too complicated for him. A few days after the Greek junta threw all pretence aside and attacked the government of Cyprus in strength with tanks and artillery, Dr Kissinger told a press conference that, 'The information was not lying around in the streets.' Some years afterwards, he told *Time* magazine that, 'If I had ever had twelve hours and been able to pick out an intelligence report, I would have seen that the situation needed attention.'

In as much as these and other statements represent a claim by Kissinger to have been taken off guard by the July 1974 coup, they are direct lies.

In the broadest possible sense, he cannot, as National Security Advisor or as Secretary of State have been unaware of United States policy favouring the partition of Cyprus since 1964. In a sense hardly less broad, he cannot, as Secretary of State, have been unaware of American commitments to the Greek junta, or of that junta's commitment to the removal or overthrow of Makarios. In the specific sense of day-to-day policy, he may have ignored but cannot have forgotten the many warnings that he was given as early as March 1974.

Here, one must be pedantic. The United States administration knew of the impending coup against President Makarios and, at the very least, did nothing to prevent it. To be specific:

1. On 7 June 1974, the *National Intelligence Daily*, essential breakfast reading for all senior State Department, Pentagon and national security officials, quoted an American field report dated 3 June which stated that:

> Ioannides claimed that Greece is capable of removing Makarios and his key supporters from power in twenty-four hours with little if any blood being shed and without EOKA assistance. The Turks would quietly acquiesce to the removal of Makarios, a key enemy. . . Ioannides stated that if Makarios decided on some type of extreme provocation against Greece to obtain a tactical advantage, he is not sure whether he should merely pull the Greek troops out of Cyprus and let Makarios fend for himself, or remove Makarios once and for all and have Greece deal directly with Turkey over Cyprus's future. [This statement and its contents have since been authenticated before Congress by CIA Athens staff serving at the relevant time.]

2. It still took until 29 June for Kissinger to respond to this alert. He approved a 'for-the-record' cable to the US ambassador, Henry Tasca, instructing him to tell Brigadier Ioannides that America opposed any adventure in Cyprus. 'The instruction,' drily noted the House Select Committee on Intelligence in 1976, 'was only partially heeded.' To be exact, ambassador Tasca refused to pass it on. Ioannides had no constitutional standing except as head of the Military Police. Why should a

dignified ambassador of a Great Power deal with him? The fact
that Ioannides was effective ruler of Greece was not deemed
relevant, and might not have been except that the United States
had helped to put him there and keep him there. No other
admonition to Ioannides is on record.

3. As the House Select Committee on Intelligence observed
in its 1976 report:

> Tasca, assured by the CIA station chief that Ioannides would
> *continue* to deal only with CIA, and not sharing the State
> Department Desk Officer's alarm, was content to pass a
> message to the Greek leader indirectly. . . It is clear,
> however, that the embassy took no steps to underscore for
> Ioannides the depth of concern over a Cyprus coup attempt.
> This episode, the exclusive CIA access to Ioannides, Tasca's
> indications that he may not have seen all important messages
> to and from the CIA station, Ioannides's suggestions of US
> acquiescence, and Washington's well-known coolness to
> Makarios have led to public speculation that either US
> officials were inattentive to the reports of the developing
> crisis or simply allowed it to happen.

4. Thomas Boyatt, who was then the Cyprus desk officer in
the State Department, whose 'alarm' is the alarm referred to
above, and who had served as a diplomat on the island, warned
consistently of a coup and of the inevitable Turkish response to
it. He confirmed that the junta was planning an attack on
Cyprus. Boyatt recapitulated the long involvement of the junta
in plots against Makarios. His pre-coup memoranda were
classified as secret and have never been released. After the
invasion, he was at first forbidden by Kissinger to testify before
Congress, and was finally allowed to do so in order to avoid
being cited for contempt. His evidence was taken in 'Executive
Session', with the room cleared of staff, reporters and visitors.

5. On 1 July 1974 three senior officials of the Greek Foreign
Ministry, all of them known to be moderate on the Cyprus
issue, publicly tended their resignations.

6. On 3 July President Makarios issued an open letter to
General Phaidon Gizikis, the puppet President of Ioannides's

regime. The letter, which sent a shock through western Europe as well as Greece and Cyprus, was extremely audacious and unambiguous. Its decisive paragraph, rounding off a litany of complaints against the junta, read as follows:

> In order to be absolutely clear, I say that the cadres of the military regime of Greece support and direct the activities of the EOKA-B terrorists. . . It is also known, and an undeniable fact, that the opposition Cyprus press, which supports the criminal activities of EOKA-B and which has its source of financing in Athens, receives guidance from those in charge of the General Staff office and the branch of the Greek Central Intelligence Agency in Cyprus.

Makarios did not believe in using silky ambivalence unless he really had to. He therefore added that: 'I have more than once so far felt, and in some cases I have touched, a hand invisibly extending from Athens and seeking to liquidate my human existence.'

He ended his open letter in spirited fashion, calling for the withdrawal of the Greek officers who had been subverting and poisoning the National Guard. Here was the 'type of extreme provocation' which Ioannides knew, when he talked to the CIA in Athens, that his own Cyprus policy was inviting and even necessitating.

All this is to say that Kissinger lied both by *suppressio veri* and *suggestio falsi*. The information was not just 'lying around on the streets' of Athens and Nicosia, it was also littering the corridors of the State Department. Yet at no stage was the Greek ambassador to Washington summoned, and at no stage did Kissinger display anything but an unpleasant insouciance when presented with warnings. (He told one senior staffer who protested at his callous indifference that: 'I don't want any goddamn social science lectures.') The Greek Cypriot daily *Apogevmatini* (*Afternoon*) outdid the mighty Secretary of State in its edition on 5 July. It stated confidently in an editorial that the Greek junta was planning:

> A broad coupist action to take place in the next few days

supported by certain military circles in co-operation with units of the National Guard and EOKA-B groups, for the purpose of seizing power. This coupist action has been planned in such a way that it formally releases senior military personnel or Greek army circles from any responsibility. . . If the plan succeeds, the government will be taken over by a certain person who has already been chosen and who, in substance, will be the puppet for a transitional period. Naturally, it is understood that the partition of Cyprus will be achieved through the coup plan with the understanding that the Turks have their plans prepared for such a golden opportunity.

Did the Cypriot journalist who penned that editorial really know more than Henry Kissinger – or less?

The date of 15 July 1974 was the ninth anniversary of the constitutional coup which ousted George Papandreou from the Prime Ministership of Greece – at least in part because he defended Makarios from the extreme Right. The irony was unintended. The junta was in a hurry, and had once again been caught unawares by the Archbishop's 'going public'. This had given him time in the past; granted him a stay of execution. On this occasion, it panicked his foes into an earlier strike than they had planned. But, when it came, it was no less ghastly for having been anticipated.

The Coup

A writer should be careful about using the well-worn metaphor of 'Greek tragedy'. Many superficial accounts of the Cyprus crisis have used the term ineptly or incorrectly, satisfied with the resonance of the word in any Hellenic context and glad of the opportunity to employ it. The coup in Cyprus was not a 'classic' tragedy. It was not the outcome of rash human acts, misunderstood by their authors but monitored by the Fates. It was the result of human design, the consequences of which were perfectly understood by at least some of the actors. But it is true to say that, from the moment the first salvoes were fired at the

Presidential Palace, every other 'tragic' consequence was more or less assured.

The consequences were not precisely those which the rattled putschists had intended. This was one of those moments in history where the life or death of one individual make all the difference. The junta men banked on their ability to kill Makarios and to offer his cadaver as a symbol of goodwill to Turkey and to the United States. A relatively orderly division of the spoils would then follow, with something for everybody. But, for that to work even on the best prognosis, the executors of the coup would have to be rational. And rational they were not. The luckless footsoldiers of the operation had been told that they were fighting for *enosis* and, once out of their cages, behaved as if that was their objective. This, in itself, was enough to give the ordinary Turkish Cypriots vivid memories of 1963. But two other developments put events beyond the control of their originators.

The first of these was the least predictable. In spite of everything, including heavy and vicious shelling of the Presidential Palace, Makarios survived. Not only did he survive, he escaped. His supporters put up quite a resistance to cover his flight, while the new junta-controlled Cyprus radio broadcast gloating announcements of his death. With Makarios alive, the junta could not move to its next stage.

The second miscalculation was just as telling. The junta installed, as President, Nicos Sampson. Sampson (see page 39) was a well-known thug and killer; a man devoid of education or culture and, as we have seen, a relentless hater of Turks. His name alone was enough to send a *frisson* through the Turkish Cypriot quarter, which remembered him from 1963 and which had been frightened since by the lurid and violent tone of his newspapers. The British, too, had no cause to love him. His exploits, even as a 'freedom-fighter' in the 1950s, had not been savoury. There was thus no chance that either of the other two guarantor powers would contemplate recognizing such a person in office.

All the evidence points to Sampson's having been a last-minute choice. He was, after all, more likely to provoke an angry Turkish invasion than an 'understanding' about partition.

He lacked polish and had no experience in government. Many other Greek Cypriot Rightists of the more respectable kind were approached (the law of libel forbids direct mention of names; Cyprus still has a British legal system). But Makarios's open letter had shaken their nerve, and the frenzy of Ioannides was not to their taste. By bringing forward the date of the coup, and by appearing so obviously responsible for it, the junta was forced to find somebody cast more in its own image – someone, in fact, who would be regarded even by quite entrenched conservatives with plain horror. The option of General Grivas was closed to them – he had died of a heart attack a few weeks previously. Sampson was chosen *faute de mieux* – the bottom of the barrel.

Dr Kissinger, however, treated him with respect and almost with courtesy. Compare, for instance, the different receptions accorded to the two Dimitrious. Nicos Dimitriou was the ambassador of Cyprus to Washington. His brother Dimis became Nicos Sampson's 'Foreign Minister' on the day of the coup. Dr Kissinger received the ambassador on the first day of the Emergency, and insulted him with jokes while failing to offer any condolences on the reported death of his President. In Nicosia, ambassador Rodger Davies received Dimis Dimitriou as 'Foreign Minister' – the only envoy to do so. In Washington, as day succeeded day, Kissinger's press spokesman, ambassador Robert Anderson, reflected his employer's readiness to do business with the new regime, and his refusal to admit what was obvious to everyone else.

For example, Kissinger's State Department never agreed that the coup in Cyprus, which had been carried out with tanks and heavy artillery under the command of Greek officers, was an interference by Athens. 'No. In our view there has been no outside intervention,' was the official Anderson statement when challenged on this very point. At the same time, most of the governments in western Europe were stating what was clear – that the Greek Colonels had mounted an unpardonable intrusion into the affairs of another state. The death of Grivas meant that not even EOKA-B had a token Cypriot commander.

This hypocrisy on Kissinger's part was deplorable for three

reasons. First, he and the State Department were well aware that the Greek junta was responsible for the coup; and they had also been aware of the planning for it. Even if one takes Dr Kissinger's tepid cable of 29 June at its face value, it makes an official lie out of his later disclaimers. The cable had, after all, explicitly recognized that Athens was preparing to move against Makarios.

Second, Kissinger could only, by his pretended innocence, have given the badly worried Greek dictators the feeling that they were not alone in the world, and might get away with it. Third, it made it much easier for Turkey to act unilaterally and to claim that the situation gave her no choice but to do so. A concerted move by the Western democracies to isolate the junta would have made such a Turkish attack very hard to justify. And, perhaps for that reason, no such move was ever made. The Turkish card was to be kept in reserve.

Collusion

For the remainder of July and August 1974, the Cypriots yet again had no choice but to let others be the actors in the drama of their own country. There was a brief and heroic resistance to the Sampson coup, in which members of Makarios's security forces and the militants of the Socialist Party distinguished themselves. The fighting, as Mr Denktash admitted at the time, was confined to the Greek Cypriots: Sampson's forces left the Turks alone for the time being and many Greek Cypriot dissidents took shelter with their Turkish neighbours in a gratifying moment of fraternity. But the Turkish Cypriots could not be expected to believe that Sampson was their friend; they had to ask what, if he could do this to Greeks, would he do to them? They withdrew, in large numbers, into their enclaves and turned on the Turkish radio.

Here it ought to be stressed that the Greek junta planned to share Cyprus with *Turkey*. It had never had a policy for the Turkish *Cypriots*, and its own demented logic had forced it to rely on the most chauvinistic Greeks; the ones least likely to convince Turkish Cypriots, as opposed to Turkish generals, of

anything. So, before considering the disastrous course that
matters actually took, one ought to remember that there was
the possibility for Greeks and Turks to coexist, *as Cypriots*, in
spite of all the years of intrigue and foreign meddling.

In his book *The Road to Bellapais*, which is generally
speaking the most naïvely pro-Turkish account of the Cyprus
problem yet to be published, Professor Pierre Oberling has the
following rather striking passage:

> Already by 1969, relations between the Greek Cypriots and
> the Turkish Cypriots had so dramatically improved that
> when a tornado struck the Turkish Cypriot quarter of
> Limassol, Makarios inspected the damage and promised the
> victims that his government would provide them with all that
> was necessary to rebuild their homes. However, while
> relations between the Greek Cypriots and the Turkish
> Cypriots were improving, those between the Greek Cypriot
> and Greek governments were steadily deteriorating. . . The
> junta was determined to achieve *enosis*; the acquisition of
> Cyprus would crown its rule with glory and legitimize its
> continued existence. But Makarios now seemed determined
> to barter it away for the sake of achieving a rapprochement
> with the Turkish Cypriots and restoring the unity of his
> long-divided nation.

This generous observation by Professor Oberling (the ac-
knowledgements of whose book contain only official Turkish
sources and not a single Greek) is one that must be borne in
mind. In describing the second stage of the 1974 catastrophe,
one has to employ the shorthand of 'Greeks' and 'Turks'. But
the crisis did *not* grow out of tension between them, which was
slowly waning. It grew out of the policies of those who did not
want Cypriot harmony, and who feared that it would lead to
'Communism'. The Greek junta provided all the vindication
that Turkish extremists could reasonably have wished. All the
enemies of Cypriot independence now saw their chance.

The events of the next few days are somewhat kaleidoscopic.
They can best be understood if they are considered capital by
capital: Washington, London, Athens, Ankara and Geneva.

Invasion and Evasions

Washington: Dr Kissinger's romance with the Sampson mini-junta, and with its Athenian parent, became more difficult to conduct once it was obvious that Makarios had survived. There was undisguised gloom on the fifth floor of the State Department when it became known that he had escaped and been flown, by British military plane, to Malta and then to London. It also became obvious that Turkey would be anxious to take advantage of the vacuum, even to fill it by invasion. Makarios had very few friends or defenders in Washington, because of his obdurate independence down the years. Moreover, the Greek-American leadership had been wooed by Nixon and (often very willingly) exploited in its patriotism by the 'Hellenic' slogans of the junta. There were very few people, in this most crucial capital, who were prepared to intercede for the Archbishop.

However, I have the testimony of Elias P. Demetracopoulos, who was at all material times in touch with the State Department and the Senate Foreign Relations Committee. Demetracopoulos, a distinguished Greek journalist, had warned of the coup in Greece before 1967, and had left Athens after his predictions came true. He established himself in Washington, becoming a major one-man crusade against the dictatorship. He survived several attempts to deport and kidnap him and to blacken his name, with allegations of subversive intent, by a deliberate campaign of disinformation. (In one of the few happy footnotes to this story, Demetracopoulos secured a full retraction of all the allegations made against him by Nixon's Watergate plumbers and the CIA. See the *New York Times* of 29 September 1983 and the *Washington Post* of 20 October 1983.)

Demetracopoulos, whose sources in his native Greece were good and who had a reputation for shrewd prognostication, got wind of the Cyprus coup in early June 1974. He took his evidence to Senator William Fulbright, then Chairman of the Senate Foreign Relations Committee, a close friend and defender of Kissinger, and perhaps the most powerful man in Congress at that time. Fulbright agreed to approach Dr Kissinger with a plan to avert the coup. This would serve

American interest, he argued with the help of a Demetracopoulos briefing, because it would restore the prestige that had
been tarnished by association with the junta. It would also
enhance American influence in Cyprus, and might forestall a
war in the eastern Mediterranean. Kissinger refused to act, on
the peculiar grounds that he could not intervene in Greek
internal affairs while the Nixon administration was resisting
pressure to link US–Soviet trade to the free emigration of
Russian Jewry.

So, having failed to head off the coup (and having inciden-
tally made further nonsense of Kissinger's later protestations of
surprise at it), Demetracopoulos attempted to minimize its
consequences. Again with the co-operation of Senator Fulbright, he sought to have the escaped Makarios invited to
Washington *as President of Cyprus*. At the time, Kissinger and
his spokesman Robert Anderson were steadily refusing to say
whether or not they recognized the Makarios government. On
18 July, ambassador Anderson was asked directly if the United
States was moving to recognize Nicos Sampson, as had been
repeatedly reported and as seemed likely. Anderson declined to
deny the reports. He was then asked about Makarios's
forthcoming visit to Washington. Was Kissinger seeing Makarios on the following Monday 22 July 'as a private citizen, as
Archbishop, or as President of Cyprus?' Came the answer, with
all the gravity of the State Department, 'He's meeting with
Archbishop Makarios on Monday.' At least there was no
question of challenging his ecclesiastical authority.

This was precisely the ambiguity against which Demetracopoulos and Fulbright were contending. Having telephoned
Kissinger on 17 July (the transcript of the call is retained by
Kissinger; a move which is being disputed in the American
courts) they arranged for Makarios to be invited, as President
of Cyprus, by both the Senate Foreign Relations and House
Foreign Affairs Committees. After this, Kissinger could hardly
do otherwise than extend the same courtesy. And then came
another suggestion, even more audacious. It was made by
Demetracopoulos and conveyed personally to Kissinger by
Senator Fulbright. How would the Secretary of State react if
Makarios were to invite the Sixth Fleet to pay a goodwill visit to

the ports of Cyprus? After all the controversy over home-porting the fleet in Athens, how could Kissinger refuse an unsolicited invitation? Such a move, of course, would have the effect of repudiating the Greek junta and obviating the need for a Turkish military invasion.

Kissinger's reply was not long delayed. He would not hear of the Sixth Fleet going to Cyprus, but he would agree to receive Makarios. He would not say whether or not it would be as President (at the last moment, it was). Interestingly enough, it was never objected that it would be *technically* difficult to deploy the Sixth Fleet on a goodwill visit. After all the fuss about home-porting and the need for a quick reaction in the Levant, that would have been ridiculous.

With Makarios alive, and as the Greek junta's position eroded, there came definite symptoms of a shift towards Turkey on the part of the administration. Once again, there was the peculiar spectacle of intelligence agencies saying that they knew nothing, and of military headquarters saying that they could do nothing. This was not the standard Nixon–Kissinger style. Even when caught in the thickets of Watergate, they had managed quite complex interventions in Chile and Indochina. To act in the case of Cyprus, however, seemed beyond them.

Robert Ellsworth, Assistant Secretary of Defense for International Security Affairs, told Demetracopoulos, and others who expressed concern that the Greek attack on Cyprus would be followed by a Turkish one, that Turkey did not have the capacity to invade. She was, he claimed, short of landing craft. This claim is made transparently absurd with hindsight, but it was in fact absurd even at the time. Turkey had been readying an invasion force since before the 15 July coup. John 'Jack' Maury, who had been CIA station chief in Athens during the 1967 coup, and who was in 1974 Assistant Secretary of Defense for Legislative Affairs, knew of these preparations.* Even as

* In 1982, as President of the Association of Former Intelligence Officers, Maury told a sympathetic interviewer, for direct quotation, that, 'I find nothing morally wrong in assassination. The problem is that you're never sure that the person who succeeds is going to be an improvement on the one who's gone; that's the difficulty.' Indeed. (Brian Freemantle, *CIA*. Stein and Day, New York, 1984.)

far back as 1964, a decade previously, when they issued their
stern warning to President Inonu, Lyndon Johnson and his
advisers had not doubted the *ability* of the Turks to invade. A
sentence from Johnson's famous letter of June 1964 looked
more significant than it had then:

> Your government is required to obtain the United States'
> consent in the use of military assistance for purposes other
> than those for which such assistance was intended. . . I must
> tell you in all candor that the United States cannot agree to
> the use of any United States-supplied military equipment for
> a Turkish intervention in Cyprus *under present circum-
> stances.* [italics mine]

In 1964 LBJ had been concerned about the possibility that
the Soviet Union would intervene against Turkey. In 1974 there
was no such concern. Ankara took care to keep Moscow
informed of its intentions. And, given Soviet hostility to the
Greek junta and its American backers, there could be scant
grounds for their opposing an operation ostensibly designed to
thwart their immediate objectives. The opportunity to exploit a
fissure within NATO also presented itself. This was one crisis
which the Soviet Union was happy to sit out. Or, as a Turkish
diplomat in Washington translated the changed situation, 'We
could no longer be scared off by threats of the Soviet
bogeyman.'

On 19–20 July, the first Turkish shock troops landed on the
northern shore of Cyprus. On 22 July, the day Kissinger met
with President Makarios, the Athens junta began to collapse.
And when it began to collapse, it collapsed very quickly;
disproving in the process seven years of Panglossian American
propaganda about its durability and popularity. In his study of a
much more impressive structure of rule, Montesquieu wrote in
1734 that, 'if a particular cause, like the accidental result of a
battle, has ruined a state, there was a general cause which made
the downfall of this state ensue from a single battle'. The Greek
junta was hated, and was corrupt to the bones. It would have
fallen anyway, and probably in a year or two. But Cyprus was at
least the proximate cause of its ruin. The Greek dictators,

caught in a trap of their own making, expired as cynically as they had ruled. They dumped the entire crisis into the lap of the civilians they had excoriated so long, agreed to the return of Constantine Karamanlis from his exile in Paris, and surrendered power. From the warped perspective of Dr Kissinger, the restoration of democracy to Greece was a nuisance and a distraction (see page 150). But it did simplify matters. He no longer had to deal with rival clients. The way to agreement with Turkey, so long the Cinderella of his statecraft, now lay open and relatively unimpeded.

London: The late Richard Crossman, a distinguished politician and essayist and something of a specialist on British cabinet government, made a small but interesting entry in his *Diaries of a Cabinet Minister* for 28 July 1967. As Lord President of the Council and Leader of the House of Commons, he had attended a meeting of the Defence and Overseas Policy Committee of the cabinet:

> We then turned to an astonishing paper on Cyprus, a copy of which I had discovered among the huge mass of bumf which was provided for this meeting of the committee. This paper advised that if on the instructions of the Greek government the Greek army in Cyprus staged a coup against Makarios in order to achieve *enosis*, we should dissent from it but prevent our troops from getting engaged in any hostilities. Denis Healey and I were the only two people there who had noticed this extraordinary proposal. A Commonwealth country is attacked by a Fascist dictatorship which tries to upset its constitutional government and though we have 15,000 armed men there we stand aside. . . What made it even more astonishing was that this proposal was part of a huge paper recommending that we should make our presence in Cyprus virtually permanent. I suppose it's explained by the fact that authority is divided between the Foreign Office and the Commonwealth Office, but when I asked the Foreign Secretary afterwards he said, 'After all, the Cypriots have got a very bad record of voting with the Russians in all UN matters' – as though that settled the issue.

Seven years later, when the predictions implied in that exchange finally came true, the British government (which contained the same senior personnel as had the 1967 one, including Harold Wilson, Denis Healey and James Callaghan) affected complete surprise. They also sought to avoid their obligations under the 1960 Treaty of Guarantee; a treaty, be it noted, which the British rather than the Cypriots had insisted upon. Arnold Smith, then Secretary General of the Commonwealth, recalled in his 1981 memoir, *Stitches in Time*, how the evasion was justified:

> When I heard the news of the coup, I was in Ghana lunching with General Acheampong, and actually had an appointment to fly overnight to Cyprus for a working lunch with Makarios the next day. Instead, I flew back to London and at once urged the British government to press a resolution in the UN Security Council calling for the immediate resignation of Sampson and restoration of Makarios, with a swift deadline for the UN peacekeeping forces already on the island to act in support. No UN peacekeeping operation could have been easier. The Soviet Union was opposed to the Greek junta, the US Sixth Fleet was nearby; the British also had bases on the island. The junta would have fallen, to the joy of the Greek people; the Turks would have been placated, Cyprus would have been restored to peace, and the West would have gained some credit. The British told me they would not act in the Security Council unless Kissinger agreed in advance. Instead, they hesitated while Kissinger sent his envoy to talk with the Greek Colonels and the Turkish government. The opportunity was lost, for within five days the Turkish army invaded Cyprus. The Greek junta fell, Sampson resigned – and Makarios was eventually restored – but at the fearful cost of dividing Cyprus far more deeply than before.

These two quotations from senior participants more or less sum up the British role in the betrayal of Cyprus. Ever since they had surrendered sovereignty over the island in 1960, the British had sought to pass on the responsibility to the United States. A declining imperial power which had, until a few years previously, insisted that Cyprus was its exclusive preserve, now sought to dispose of it by any means.

Three days after the Sampson coup, the Turkish Prime Minister Bulent Ecevit flew to London. He was joined there by Joseph Sisco, Kissinger's luckless understrapper in a 'shuttle diplomacy' which the great man did not wish, for reasons of his own, to embark upon himself. Under-secretary Sisco discovered what Ecevit and Arnold Smith had already found – that the British government was not prepared to meet its obligations as a guarantor power. This, as has since been established, was because Kissinger had told them to leave it to him. (I shall not easily forget how James Callaghan, then Her Majesty's Principal Secretary of State for Foreign and Commonwealth Affairs, told me that his guiding policy was the belief in Kissinger's ability to bring about peace.)

Bulent Ecevit had two motives in flying to London. The first was the need to demonstrate that Turkey had exhausted every option short of war. The second was to contain his eager and anxious General Staff who, once authorized, might slip the leash of civilian authority altogether. He succeeded in the first much better than the second. But, with Greece exposed as an aggressor and Britain studiously copying the Kissinger line of 'see no evil', he got his green light.

Athens: The scene in Greece's capital, meanwhile, was one of appalling squalor and chaos. In Washington a State Department official, who learned from a Greek diplomat of the escape of Makarios, had remarked on the telephone, 'How inconvenient.' He could afford to be laconic. At the headquarters of the junta, there was something more closely resembling hysteria. The Greek embassy in London later supplied me with the transcript of a telephone conversation between Brigadier Ioannides and Nicos Sampson. It took place the day after the coup in Nicosia.

IOANNIDES: I see that the old s— has escaped. Where could he be now?

SAMPSON: On the mountains, heading towards Kykkos [site of the monastic headquarters of the Cypriot Orthodox Church]. I hope to have him arrested within two or three hours.

IOANNIDES: Nicky, I want his head. You shall bring it to me yourself, OK Nicky?

After this Mafia chat, the two defenders of the West got off the line. Within twenty-four hours, their subordinates were in touch again. The nervous Cypriots at one end of the telephone had to confess that 'the old s—' was still at large. They needed perhaps one day to finish him. 'You haven't got a day!' shrieked the voice from Athens, 'we're under great pressure from outside.' The Greek word employed for 'outside' was *apexo*, which means 'abroad'.

There is no absolutely watertight proof that Brigadier Ioannides had guarantees from *apexo*. We are, after all, recounting the behaviour of a near-madman. But it is certain that he *thought* that he had such guarantees. There was, too, some method in his madness. American policy, as Professor Theodore Couloumbis has so elegantly put it, was concerned that Greece and Turkey not wage an intra-NATO war. American policy, on the other hand, did nothing to prevent and something to facilitate a Greek military move on Cyprus. *Ergo*, as the professor writes:

> A war could have been excluded with certainty only through a prearrangement of Greeks (the junta) and Turks to eliminate Makarios and to partition Cyprus. If such an agreement did not exist (and there is no contrary evidence to date), then one can speculate that Ioannides was somehow led to 'assume' that the Turks would not have reacted to his anti-Makarios putsch, and that he naïvely went along with such a presumption.

That is to put it mildly, but firmly. Brigadier Ioannides has stated many times, through his trial lawyers and through other conduits, that he held such an 'assumption'. Since such testimony tends to incriminate him more rather than less (he is currently serving a life sentence for his many crimes), it may at least be placed in evidence. It also explains his extreme anxiety that the Sampson coup be a 'success', at least in the sense that it physically destroyed Makarios. Without the head of 'the old s—', the usefulness of the gallant Ioannides was at an end.

For a brief moment, like the namesake of his deputy Sampson, Ioannides considered bringing the roof down with him. Realizing that the Turks were not going to co-operate in his fiasco, and seeing that the Kissinger faction was in the process of shifting its allegiance to the ascendant power, he ordered a general, *kamikaze* attack on Turkey. At this, like Prussian Junkers belatedly disdainful of an Austrian corporal, the Greek senior officers baulked. Fighting unarmed civilians was one thing. Fighting the Turks in a losing cause was another. Moreover, Joseph Sisco had been in town, seeking to dampen the enthusiasm his chief had helped to encourage. His mission had been an abject failure, in that it had been launched after rather than before the coup. But it had the effect of opening an escape route for the less committedly ideological military men. They took it with tremendous gratitude.

It hardly needs to be added that the Cyprus junta fell on the same day as the Greek one. How could it have been otherwise? It does need to be added, however, (because the obvious is so often overlooked) that Brigadier Ioannides resigned only temporarily. Disgusted with the near-mutinous cowardice of his Chiefs of Staff, and contemptuous of the civilian rule which they proposed as a means of saving their own skins, he stamped out of their councils. He was sure that the resulting disorder would bring him back, and he did make one or two attempts to return. But they were fruitless, because without American backing Ioannides was a stringless marionette. Greek democracy was thereby partially restored, but at the cost of a bloodbath in Cyprus.

A democratic Greece did not mean a Greece that had lost all sense of commitment to Cyprus. Shortly after Constantine Karamanlis had returned to Athens, and during the volatile period when, because of the fear of a Ioannides counter-coup, he had to sleep in a different place every night, he telephoned Evangelos Averoff. Averoff, his Defence Minister, (and today the leader of the opposition in parliament) had been the conservative politician closest to the junta but had always refused to endorse it. It was at his initiative that Karamanlis had been recalled to rescue the situation. The telephone call was a serious one. Did Averoff believe, asked Karamanlis, that

Cyprus could still be saved? To be exact, did he believe that if
the two of them embarked for the island from Crete, and
announced in advance that they were doing so, the Turks would
bomb the ship? It emerged, as Averoff was later to tell the
Greek parliament, that Karamanlis was prepared to risk their
lives to go, with Cretan troops, to save what could be saved
from the junta's folly. Averoff advised against the move,
because of Turkey's command of the air and her ingrained
suspicion of Greek motives. But the very notion illustrated
the intensity of feeling, even among conservative Greeks, for
the island and the people that had been so callously expended.
That concern, among others, has been vital in the political
radicalization that has taken place in Greece since 1974.

Ankara: In his book *Thirty Hot Days in Cyprus*, which
describes the Turkish view of the Cyprus crisis, the Establishment journalist Mehmet Ali Birand describes a conversation
between Bulent Ecevit and his naval commander-in-chief. The
Turkish invasion fleet had put to sea from the ports of
Alexandretta and Mersin, as it had done on previous occasions,
such as 1967. At a special meeting, the General Staff had shown
Ecevit contingency plans for invading Cyprus. There was one
for every month of the year, allowing for changes in weather,
and there were two alternative bridgehead sites at Famagusta
and Kyrenia. Unlike in the past, there was a power vacuum in
Greece and disorder among the Greek Cypriots. Most crucially,
there was the fact that Washington no longer had any pressing
reason to oppose an invasion. This was the moment for which
the Turkish General Staff had been planning, and waiting, for
years. Would Bulent Ecevit, the poet manqué and social
democrat, who had quarrelled with their domestic political
ambitions in the past, hesitate to implement the plan? As
Birand tells it, four days after the Sampson coup Ecevit's naval
commander, Admiral Karacan, said to him: 'Mr Prime Minister, if we turn back from Cyprus as before I won't be able to
remain naval commander-in-chief – and you won't be able to
remain Prime Minister.'
   This remark, and its implications, more or less encapsulate
the Turkish position. The state of affairs in Ankara was far less

complicated than it was in any of the other capitals concerned. For the previous decade and a half, Turkish military preponderance had been offset by political and diplomatic weakness. Now, these constraints were dissolved. Moreover Ecevit, as leader of a centre-Left party, depended on the indulgence of his conservative coalition partners, and of the generals who had surrendered power to him only some two years previously. The outcome was never in doubt, although among some of the more seasoned elder statesmen there was concern that Turkey might isolate herself internationally. But, once the first invasion was ordered, the generals knew that a second, decisive invasion would have to follow.

Joseph Sisco might just as well have stayed in Washington. His visit to Ankara, which took place between 19 and 20 July, was utterly fruitless. His efforts to implore restraint were lame, and he was not empowered even to hint of any United States disapproval of, let alone retaliation for, an invasion. Back in Athens, Mr Sisco found that his employer Dr Kissinger had left him with no leverage there either. All he could do was bleat that if Greece showed restraint, then Turkey might be induced to do the same. There were three objections to this double-bluff. One: Turkey had already begun, on 20 July, to bombard Cyprus and to land formations of parachutists. Two: the Greek junta was collapsing in a welter of mania. Three: because American policy was so wanting in skill, in principle and in synchronization, nobody any longer trusted the good offices of Kissinger's emissaries. He had managed to offend or alarm all participant nations in the dispute – even a few timorous British spokesmen felt safe enough to say in private that they regretted his alternating energy and indifference. The question became – what could he salvage? The answer was – at least an understanding with the Turks. The site of the understanding was to be Geneva.

In preparing for such an outcome Mr Ecevit was, it must be said, very scrupulous. 'His' forces landed in Cyprus with the ostensible justification of the 1960 Treaty of Guarantee. Article Four of the said treaty provides that, 'In so far as common or concerted action may not prove possible, each of the three Guaranteeing Powers reserves the right to take action with the sole aim of re-establishing the state of affairs created by the present treaty.' This permission for unilateral action (inserted, significantly, at Turkish insistence in 1960) is, however, governed by another article which states that if the Republic of Cyprus can no longer ensure, 'the maintenance of its independence, territorial integrity and security, as well as respect for its Constitution', the three guarantors must consult together 'with respect to the representations or measures necessary to secure observance'. It might be argued that Turkey was free under Article Four, given that the Greek junta had subverted Makarios and that Britain had opted to abstain. What cannot be argued is that Turkey had as its objective the larger aim – independence and territorial integrity – which the treaty expressly stipulates. Geneva, where so many essays in international understanding and so many efforts against international piracy have come to grief, was to be the setting for this distinction to be made plain.

Geneva: There were two Geneva conferences, both of them foredoomed. The first, which took place at the request of the United Nations Security Council, involved only the foreign ministers of Greece, Turkey and Great Britain, respectively Mr George Mavros, Mr Turan Gunes, and Mr James Callaghan. It took place between 25 and 30 July 1974, during a very questionable 'ceasefire' on the island. It determined that the ceasefire should be observed, that negotiations should be carried on, and that both Greek and Turkish forces should desist from bullying or occupying the territory of, respectively, Turkish and Greek Cypriots. Finally, it determined on another meeting, at which Greek and Turkish Cypriot representatives should also be present. The second meeting was set for 8 August. The Turkish army employed the intervening week by shipping in heavy reinforcements to its salient on the north coast of the island, and by favourably adjusting the edges of that salient. By the time of the second Geneva conference, then, a certain amount of Turkish 'fact-creating' had already been accomplished.

Geneva II took place under the permanent threat of another Turkish advance. The United States government, which was not formally represented at the conference but which exerted the largest influence on all the governments which were represented there, made its own position known at a critical stage.* On 13 August 1974 Dr Kissinger conveyed to the deadlocked participants the following message: 'We recognize that the position of the Turkish community requires considerable improvement and protection. We have supported a greater degree of autonomy for them. The parties are negotiating on one or more Turkish autonomous areas.'

There followed some pieties about the inadvisability of military action by any party. But note the rapidity and the significance of the change of tone. Until one month previously, the Nixon administration had been a close ally of the Greek junta and of the EOKA-B bandits. It had refused to condemn the Sampson coup, which was carried out by the most extreme anti-Turkish elements. It had declined to charge the Greek junta with engineering it. A similarly bold statement about Turkish Cypriot rights, made on the day of the Sampson coup, could have contributed to the junta's isolation and could even have allowed for the concerted international action called for by the Commonwealth and Arnold Smith. Instead, the United States chose to invoke Turkish rights only when Turkey, not Greece, had become the aggressor. Washington also made clear, as the British Foreign Secretary James Callaghan reported to Geneva, that it would not oppose Turkish military action with any sanctions, and that it would not view with favour any British or Greek opposition to it. No Turkish government could have been expected to ignore this change in policy and style, or to miss the opportunity which it presented. On the morning after the Kissinger statement, the Turkish army burst out of its northern salient and began, effectively unopposed, to set about the occupation of all of northern Cyprus. The Acheson Plan was to be achieved after a fashion, but not

---

* The United States sent Assistant Secretary Arthur Hartman as observer. Richard Nixon belatedly resigned the presidency during the conference, thus accidentally inaugurating the battle between the executive and the legislative branches over the conduct of foreign policy. Cyprus was to be the first trial of strength in this new relationship. For the moment, though, Dr Kissinger's control over foreign strategy was unchallenged.

under the conditions or by the instruments which Acheson had envisaged.

It was during the Geneva Conference that Thomas Boyatt (then Director of Cypriot Affairs, State Department) wrote a memorandum which was later classified as secret by Kissinger. A crucial extract reads:

> Then on 18 July the CIA station [in Athens] with the concurrence of ambassador Tasca reported that 'The Greek military are now solidly behind strongman Brigadier General Ioannides'; 'what Ioannides has achieved for Greece on the island is parity with the Turks'; and 'any Turkish invasion of the island would unite all the Greek nationals behind Ioannides'.
>
> How wrong can you be? Within days, the Greek army had thrown out Ioannides and brought in civilians; the Turkish army had conquered northern Cyprus and the remains of the Greek army were thrown out; Greek nationals put Ioannides in jail and united behind a civilian government.

At the time of the Geneva Conference, no less than at other times previous to it, the position of the Turkish Cypriot community did indeed 'require improvement'. So did that of the Greek Cypriot population, which was not mentioned in the Kissinger memorandum. The position of both began to require urgent improvement within twenty-four hours. Until 14 August 1974, Cyprus had known every kind of medieval war, including siege and investment and crusade. It had also experienced conquest, colonization and exploitation. In living memory it had undergone guerrilla war, subversion and near-civil war. It was now to see twentieth-century war – the real thing.

IV Attila:
Intervention to Invasion/Invasion to Occupation/Occupation to Expulsion/ Expulsion to Colonization/Colonization to Annexation

> These things actually happened. That is the thing to
> keep your eye on.
> George Orwell

In the summer of 1983 a Turkish embassy spokesman in Washington told the *Washington Post* that Turkey supported the Indonesian position on East Timor at the United Nations because it saw a 'parallel' with the Turkish case in Cyprus. The spokesman was being a little ungenerous to his own government. All verifiable and independent reports show the government of Indonesia to have been guilty of near-genocide in East Timor, using the weapon of starvation, and indulging in the indiscriminate slaughter of civilians. One wonders at any government which would voluntarily associate itself with such an atrocity. The Turkish invasion of Cyprus was not as bad as the Indonesian subjugation of Timor. But it was bad enough.

Supposing that one takes the most sympathetic view of the original Turkish intervention – that it was a necessary counter-stroke to a Greek putsch – and suppose that one regards the Turkish minority as blameless in the disruptions and brutalities of the 1960s. Suppose, further, that one ignores the long and tenacious attachment of the Turkish and Turkish Cypriot leadership to partition irrespective of the majority will. Suppose, still further, that one can forget or discount the outside involvement of the British and the United States in the same cause. Put the case that there might have been – indeed, would have been – murderous attacks on Turkish Cypriots *en masse* by a consolidated Sampson leadership. Put the case that the Cyprus problem is purely a question of the security of the Turkish Cypriots. Admit that the *first* Turkish intervention of 20 July 1974 did everybody a favour by demolishing the rule of Fascism in Greece and Cyprus. Agree and allow all this, and the *second* Turkish invasion becomes more reprehensible rather than less. By the time it took place, on 14 August 1974, the Greek irredentist forces had fallen from power in both Athens and Nicosia. Negotiations were underway, and relations between the communities on the island were stable if nervous. The pretext for the original invasion had ceased to exist, and if Mr Ecevit had withdrawn his forces he would have been remembered as the man who rid Greece of the junta, saved Cyprus from its designs, and rebuilt the image of Turkey in the West. The moral and (given such an impressive demonstration of Turkish force) the actual pressure for a lasting and generous settlement with the Turkish Cypriots would have been irresistible. Instead Mr Ecevit and his generals embarked on a policy of conquest and annexation.

Many Turks feel that European opinion is, so to speak, culturally and historically biased against them. The memories of Lepanto and the gates of Vienna, the catchphrase 'Terrible Turk', the use of the term 'Little Turk' to describe obnoxious children in nursery rhymes, all these and more have created an impression of something fearful and brutish lurking in Anatolia. There is also the strangeness of Islam to most Europeans, and the vivid, terrifying accounts of what happened to Christian Bulgaria and Armenia under Turkish rule. Greeks, in particular, have a national memory of Ottoman subjugation and it is not difficult to find strong views among them about the shortcomings of Turks as a people.

All of this is deplorable. But there is no need to draw upon ancient prejudice in examining what the Turkish army did in Cyprus in August 1974. The record is a clear one, compiled for the most part by neutral outside jurists, and it shows that Turkey employed deliberate means of terror and indiscriminate cruelty. It did not do so because of something in its nature or because of the inheritance of some presumed streak of barbarism. It did so for the very modern and cold-blooded reason that it wanted territory without inhabitants. The policy was designed to make the civilian population run away, and in this it succeeded. To understand the success, one need only examine the report, adopted on 10 July 1976, of the European Commission of Human Rights. The eighteen distinguished lawyers of the commission, which was chaired by Professor J.E.S. Fawcett, a Briton, and included jurists from most of the nineteen members of the Council of Europe, spent the year between May 1975 and May 1976 preparing their report. It was thus in no sense a 'rush to judgement'. Nor was it conducted in the immediate aftermath of the invasion, when rumours and tempers were both at a high pitch. The final draft is at once meticulous and horrifying. It finds that the Turkish army engaged in the killing of civilians, in the execution of prisoners, in the torture and ill-treatment of detainees, and in organized looting, as well as in arbitrary mass detention of civilians. Revolting offences against women were also found to have been committed. (A telling fact here is that the Orthodox Church in Cyprus, for years a stern foe of abortion, was compelled to relax its rules on the termination of pregnancy because of the devastating number of rapes.)

The worst instances, and the best documented, were the shootings of unarmed civilians at the village of Palekythrou, and the treatment of 2,000 Greek Cypriot males taken as prisoners to mainland Turkey. Medical evidence taken in the last case showed deliberate malnutrition and organized sadistic mistreatment, violating all the rules of war.*

There is one consolation for the researcher who reads this and other reports, who watches the films of victims' testimony, or who talks as I have done to ordinary doctors on the island about what they were finding in their surgeries during and after those appalling days. In case after case, Greek Cypriots reported that their Turkish Cypriot neighbours came to their

---

*There are a dozen American passport-holders still missing from this period, which is testimony in itself to the Turkish army's lack of discrimination.

aid. In several instances, Cypriot Turks intervened to save women from rape, or brought food and water to those being held without either. They often, also, arranged for messages to be taken from villages that had been cut off or surrounded. None the less, the Turkish authorities chose to regard the commission as an insult to the entire Turkish nation, and rejected its findings out of hand. The commissioners were not permitted to visit the occupied north, or the Turkish mainland ports of Mersin and Adana where prisoners had been taken. The Turkish member of the commission, Professor Bulent Daver, entered a dissent to the report, in which he challenged the jurisdiction of the Republic of Cyprus and drew attention to the wrongs suffered by Turkish Cypriots in the past. But he did not contest or deny the substantive findings of the commission.

The report, of course, could examine only violations of the existing rules of war and conventions on human rights. It could not pass judgement, for example, on the use of napalm by the Turkish air force or the heavy bombing of the undefended cities of Nicosia and Famagusta. The destruction of the Athalassa mental hospital and other clinics clearly marked with the Red Cross, the ruining of the fine Armenian Melkonian Institute, the burning of the forests – these are the crimes of war rather than the crimes in war. To the population which endured both, this may seem a distinction without a difference.

Between 14 and 16 August, in a rapid and obviously well-planned advance, the Turkish forces moved to occupy thirty-four per cent of Cyprus. Over 180,000 Greek Cypriots fled their homes, for reasons which were made clear above. The advance halted on a line which was almost precisely the one proposed by Turkey as the demarcation of partition in 1965, and rejected by United Nations mediator Galo Plaza. This line put, and puts, three of the island's ports (Famagusta, Karavostassi and Kyrenia) in Turkish hands, as well as the important town of Morphou and the northern half of the capital Nicosia. The fertile agricultural plain of the Messaoria also came under Turkish control. These towns, ports and districts represented more than just one-third of Cypriot territory and population. They contained two-thirds of Cypriot tourism, two-thirds of cultivated land, sixty per cent of water resources, sixty per cent of mining and quarrying, and almost the same proportion of industrial plant.

Invasion rapidly led to consolidation. There was no pretence that Turkey was moving in response to Greek or Greek Cypriot military activity – its command of the air alone was enough to insure against that. On 22 August Mr Rauf Denktash proclaimed the establishment of an 'autonomous' Turkish Cypriot administration, thus inaugurating what was to become a consistent policy of negotiating from *faits accomplis*. And on 9 September the Turkish mainland authorities announced that 5,000 farm workers were to be sent to Cyprus as 'seasonal workers' to look after the abandoned farms and orchards. This, too, was a prefiguration of a future policy. While the Greek Cypriots were still reeling from the impact of the coup and the invasion, Turkey began to transform its 'peace-keeping' presence into an occupation.

This was accomplished in three related ways. First, the Turkish Cypriots in the south had to be induced to move to the Turkish-held north. Second, the Greek Cypriots remaining in the north had to be persuaded to move south. Third, the resulting shortfall in manpower, especially skilled manpower, had to be made up. These things had all to be done quickly; more quickly than the cumbersome machinery of international disapproval could move. Already there were signs that the United States Congress was exasperated by Kissinger's private foreign policy, and that sanctions against Turkey were being sought energetically. Most of the Turkish objectives were completed within a very short span of time. Help in this process came from three other forces, all of which we have met before. These were American cynicism, British naïveté about American cynicism, and Greek chauvinism.

When the 'ceasefire' line was drawn by Turkey on 18 August, and after a general exchange of prisoners had been agreed on 20 September, there were still many thousands of Greeks and Turks on either side of the border. The Greeks were mainly concentrated, in the number of some 11,000, in the Karpass peninsula, which forms the 'panhandle' shown on the map by the north-eastern extremity of the island. This had been by-passed in the Turkish army's dash to split the country across the middle and further to the south. The Turkish Cypriots, mainly from Paphos and Limassol at the diametrically opposed extremity of Cyprus, had taken refuge in the British Sovereign Base Area of Akrotiri. Some of them had been threatened or harshly treated by Greek Cypriot extremists, including the disbanded sweepings of the National Guard and EOKA-B, who had attempted to use them as hostages against the Turkish advance. In other scattered villages there had been killings of helpless Turkish Cypriot villagers, no less disgraceful for being 'unofficial' or performed by uniformed riff-raff 'off duty'. This was, perhaps, the last favour that EOKA-B and its junta allies were to do for the cause of partition.

In the north, harassment and cruelty were a matter of official policy, all of it designed to create a refugee mentality among the remaining Greeks. Nevertheless, the numbers were large enough to allow, on both sides, a certain solidarity in the face of attempts at 'winkling'. So the year 1975 began with Cyprus still avoiding a final separation of communities, and with Congress pressing urgently for an arms embargo on Turkey for its abuse of American 'defensive' weaponry during the invasion. Dr Kissinger was holding out strongly against any sanctions on his new ally, but it looked as if the democratic process would have its revenge on him. Turkish policy then became more active. Mr Denktash refused to discuss the return of refugees, citing it as a 'political' issue rather than a humanitarian one. He increased pressure on the United Kingdom to send the 10,000 Turkish Cypriots at Akrotiri base to Turkey, whence, he made it clear, they would be sent on to northern Cyprus to populate abandoned Greek properties. Asked whether he would count this as a concession, he was evasive. At a meeting of the NATO foreign ministers in December 1974, Dr Kissinger had urged James Callaghan to send the Akrotiri refugees to Turkey, in spite of the fact that many of them had expressed a clear preference for remaining near their old homes. Kissinger argued that this would inspire Turkish concessions and help him in his tussle with Congress over the arms embargo.

On 15 January, without consulting the government of Cyprus and without linking their departure to any reciprocal Turkish action, the British authorities sent the Turkish Cypriots to

Turkey *en masse*. Among other things, this action violated a provision in the Sovereign Bases Agreement which forbade their use as civilian airports. Mr Roy Hattersley, then Minister of State at the Foreign Office, later told the House of Commons that, 'We hoped that an act of compassion and humanity on our part would be reciprocated by the Turks in the north. In fact it was not.'

It may be doubted that the transfer of the Turkish Cypriots was 'an act of compassion and humanity' in any case. Many of them had no wish to depart. A staff report of the Refugees Subcommittee of the Senate Judiciary Committee, published in 1975, contains the following paragraphs:

> The last of the Turkish Cypriots in Paphos moved on 11 August 1975, leaving homes they had lived in for decades. The following excerpt from a despatch published in the *Washington Post* of 11 August 1975 tells the story: 'In Paphos today, where some 500 Turkish Cypriots were being transferred to the north, the main square resounded with the sobbing and wailing of elderly women abandoning their homes after a lifetime. Greek and Turkish Cypriots mingled easily with no apparent hostility toward each other. Many of the departing Turkish Cypriots handed over the keys of their homes to the Greek Cypriot refugees, with apparent pleasure, "to look after them well", as one said.'

The Paphos transfer completed the process begun at Akrotiri. Three weeks after the Akrotiri transfer, Congress imposed an arms embargo on Turkey. One week later, on 13 February 1975, Mr Denktash proclaimed the 'Turkish Federated State of Cyprus'.

So far from being 'reciprocated', to use Mr Hattersley's lazy phrasing, the British action was duplicated, but in reverse. Secure in their control of most Turkish Cypriots, the Turkish authorities began to clear the north of its hereditary Greek inhabitants. On 30 June Mr Denktash threatened to expel all the Greek Cypriots of the Karpass peninsula unless all the remaining Turkish Cypriots were moved to his zone. One month later, at a meeting in Vienna, the Greek Cypriot negotiator Glafkos Clerides agreed to this demand, securing in return a commitment from Mr Denktash that, 'The Greek Cypriots at present in the north of the island are free to stay and they will be given every help to lead a normal life, including facilities for education and for the practice of their religion, as well as medical care by their own doctors and freedom of movement in the north.'

In January of the following year (1976), the Staff Report of the Subcommittee on Refugees of the US Senate was published and contained the following sentences: 'Life among Cypriot Greeks in the north has not only not improved, it has deteriorated since the Cypriot–Turkish administration solemnly pledged in Vienna to take steps to normalize and protect their lives. . . *In no respect* has the Turkish administration fulfilled its obligation entered into at the third round of intercommunal talks.'

What was happening has been graphically described by several independent eye-witnesses as well as by the survivors themselves. Throughout the Karpass peninsula, Turkish soldiers and police set about making life insupportable for the inhabitants. Long, arbitrary curfews were imposed. Brutal and vandalistic searches, on the pretext of 'security' were commonplace. Livestock and other property was taken at gunpoint. Villagers were pointedly offered forms 'applying' for a transfer to the south. Often, the forms came already filled in and the family was simply driven to the border and dumped. One thousand, five hundred of the 9,000 or so remaining Karpassians were removed in this way, and one year after the Vienna agreement the survivors addressed a petition to Dr Kurt Waldheim, Secretary-General of the United Nations. They implored him to prevent their forcible expulsion. On 9 December Dr Waldheim reported to the United Nations that, 'from 7,371 on 5 June 1976 the Greek Cypriot population in the north decreased to 3,631 on 6 December'. Expulsions were continuing at the rate of forty each day. At that rate, the Karpass peninsula soon became almost completely empty of its former inhabitants. Today, a few Greeks remain in the village of Rizokarpasso, near the very tip of the 'panhandle'. I visited them in October 1979, without the escort on which the Turkish authorities normally insist, and found that most of them are old men, too old to move. There was an atmosphere of desolation in the village. The old men were afraid that visitors would bring trouble to the place – the exact reverse of the reception a stranger in Cyprus would usually be accorded. Police surveillance was continuous. It was evident that time would soon close the little coffee-shop where the old men sat and the church which they used.

The counterpart to the expulsion policy was one of colonization. As the Greeks were decanted or driven over the border, leaving their homes and farms and orchards, immigrants were brought in from mainland Turkey to settle and work. The undisguised purpose of this policy, which like the expulsion programme was implemented even as intercommunal negotiations were in progress, was to alter the demographic basis of the island. It is unclear to this day quite how many colonists were brought in from Anatolia, but the numbers were in the tens of thousands. Three important facts about the importation are beyond dispute. The first is that the settlement of newcomers was hasty and inept. The second is that it was connected to the plans of extremist forces in Turkey itself. The third is that it was not a success with the indigenous Turkish Cypriots.

In July 1975, the United Nations representative in Cyprus sent a letter to Dr Kurt Waldheim, in which he reported that, 'Several hundred mainland Turks are being transferred each week from Turkey and are settling in Karpass villages and villages south of the new Nicosia–Famagusta road.' Other reports from UN officials referred to the arbitrary way in which the new arrivals were allotted land and property, and the opportunities for corruption that were evident in the allocation of fictitious Cypriot passports and identity cards. Turkish Cypriot journalists and commentators also stressed that the immigrants were of a rather motley sort – unwanted in their places of origin, often with criminal records and unfamiliar with the cultural and linguistic patterns of the Turkish Cypriots. Many were unqualified for the jobs which they were ostensibly brought to the island to perform; citrus husbandry and hotel management are not as simple as they may appear to tourists.

More ominously still, many of the settlers had links with, or provided recruits for, the extremist parties based on the Turkish mainland. In the mid-seventies these parties, especially the National Action Party of Colonel Turkes, indulged in a frenzy of anti-democratic violence aimed at a 'Greater Turkey' and the establishment of a despotic system of militarist rule. An important element of this movement consisted of ex-army officers with primitive opinions, many of whom came to use occupied Cyprus as a base of operations. They helped to form a political party of a Fascist stripe, the Turkish Unity Party, which is led by former air force colonel Ismail Tezer, and which has succeeded in electing a deputy from the Famagusta district. Its programme advocates the extension of Turkish rule to the whole of Cyprus. Its public propaganda is openly addressed to Turks from the mainland, and adopts a threatening tone in addressing local political figures who speak in favour of amity with Greeks.

Incontrovertible evidence that the settlers had indeed arrived, and had not contributed greatly to the peace or the beauty of the island, was provided in May 1978. Dr Fazil Kuchuk, the veteran leader of Turkish conservatism in Cyprus; the man who cried that 'Cyprus is Turkish' in 1955, penned a series of articles in his daily newspaper *Halkin Sesi* (*Voice of the People*). At long last, northern Cyprus now *was* Turkish. But Dr Kuchuk found that it was not all he had hoped:

> We warned the officials once again. We told them that these newcomers will be a nuisance to our decent citizens; we told them to halt them before it becomes too late. They turned a deaf ear to us and did nothing. On the contrary, the newcomers were given houses, land, food and money. They were even given 'bonuses' amounting to tens of thousands of Turkish lira under the cover of settlement credits. . . We are writing bitterly because we have to. Those who opened the door without thinking are primarily responsible for the malice brought to the Turkish Cypriot community as well as to the newcomers, and they will never be able to shrug off this historic responsibility. Piling people on the island without planning has been of primary influence in the creation of the present situation on the island. We could not

let the places we had won remain empty. However, without planning and without calculation, people were brought who had sectarian conflicts among them, who lived away from each other because of blood feuds and who belonged to two different faiths. All these people were put together and 'Oriental sultanates' were established in many of our villages.

Dr Kuchuk ended his articles with the plea, in capital letters, that the Ecevit government should not turn Cyprus into a grave. He wrote that because of the authorities and the colonists, 'this paradise island is being turned into hell'. The good doctor never alluded to the sufferings of the Greek Cypriots in his article; he always was a dedicated chauvinist. It is so much the more telling, then, that he should have realized that for Turkey the Turkish Cypriots were not the main point after all.

His protest, and others like it, had some effect. Some of the settlers were quietly shipped home. But tens of thousands remained, and have been augmented by more discreet arrivals. How could it be otherwise? The brutal eviction of the Greek population *necessitated* the 'dumping operation', as it was called, of mainland colonists. And the need for haste, for action to make military conquest as far as possible irreversible, made its clumsiness inevitable. According to the original citizenship law of the 'Turkish Federated State of Kibris' – since supplanted by the 'Turkish State of North Kibris' – any member of the Turkish armed forces to have served in Cyprus, any member of the 'Turkish Resistance' and any member of their families is eligible for citizenship rights. The Turkish Cypriots are defined as members of the Great Turkish Nation.

Afterword

As early as September 1975, Mr Rauf Denktash was authorized by his supporters to drop the word 'Federated' from the 'Turkish Federated State of Kibris', and to declare 'independence'. He held this card in reserve, occasionally deploying it as a threat or using it as a bargaining point, until 15 November

1983. In a recorded interview with me in August 1983, he made clear his determination to proclaim a separate state very soon. When he did so, it came as a shock rather than a surprise (though the State Department and the Foreign Office professed themselves to be caught unawares as did, scarcely more credibly, the Turkish government in Ankara).

The declaration came in the afternoon of the day on which President Reagan had signed a billion-dollar Bill for military aid to Turkey. It came a few days after the Turkish military government had conducted a carefully managed quasi-civilian quasi-election. And it came a few days before the United States Congress was due to go into recess. Two weeks earlier, the Greek Cypriot side had accepted in writing a proposal from the United Nations for a personal initiative by Secretary-General Javier Perez de Cuellar. Mr Denktash had rejected it.

There had, obviously, been direct collusion between Mr Denktash and the Turkish military junta in the timing of the move. It is quite possible that the newly chosen civilian Prime Minister, Mr Turgut Ozal, was as innocent of knowledge as he claimed to be. If so, the fact that the army by-passed him is also of significance. But the main point of the declaration, which was for all practical purposes a declaration of *dependence* on Turkey and a declaration of secession from the Republic, was that it formally nullified Turkey's 1974 claim to have intervened in defence of the 'sovereignty and territorial integrity' of Cyprus. Like its predecessors, this Turkish move made up in decision for what it lacked in subtlety or finesse.

Desecration

Perhaps nothing illustrates the real nature of the Turkish invasion and occupation better than the pillage of northern Cyprus. It is a hard thing to say, but if the Greek Cypriot refugees were now to return to their old homes, they might well find them unrecognizable. Not only did the original landings give the signal for widespread looting, arson and vandalism, in which many Turks orgiastically celebrated their new mastery by destroying Christian and Hellenic monuments; but the resulting occupation has followed a policy of eradication. The position is made worse, and also made harder to investigate, by the related facts of widespread corruption and incompetent bureaucracy. There is something unbearable in the contemplation of this process, in the knowledge that the beauty and traditions of Cyprus are being defiled beyond repair. But the evidence for it is overwhelming, and constitutes a further proof that the Turkish plan for the island is designed to be irreversible.

The most eloquent testimony on this point comes from the Turkish Cypriot writer Mehmet Yasin. In a series of articles published in the weekly review *Olay* in April 1982, he horrified archaeologists and antiquarians who had been trying to discover what had happened to the Cypriot heritage.* It was well known that rare antiquities were turning up, often broken or disfigured, on the international black market. Very often, the pieces could be directly attributed to well-established collections, such as the Hadjiprodromou collection in Famagusta which was broken up after the invasion. But not even the Cyprus National Museum had a comprehensive account of the damage done to the national patrimony. Mehmet Yasin's report fills in a number of gaps, and his prose style also gives something of the flavour of desolation. For a lover of the island to read his articles (entitled *Perishing Cyprus*) is a very painful experience. His prologue is hauntingly recognizable as the work of a fellow-lover and a fellow-sufferer:

> This is the island of Cyprus which we now see, recognize and know. Orange groves, wheat fields, vineyards, sandstone buildings, Gothic-arched buildings, mosques, churches, bay-windowed houses, gardens of jasmine, cement houses with geraniums and flowers; Venetian, Ottoman and British coats of arms along the streets; the *moufflons*, donkeys and recently, speeding cars; old people who display olives; *halloumi* at the fairs and Friday markets; children who sell jasmine; mines and later factories; war and death all over

* In 1976, a report on the desecration of the north had been prepared for UNESCO by the Canadian authority Jacques Dalibard. Its evidence and conclusions were so damning that UNESCO decided to keep them confidential – in the hope of avoiding a rupture with Turkey.

again, living again and finally the sandbags at the borders, the listening stations of the British, radars, sieges. . .

From this evocative and tender, but ominous, beginning, Mehmet Yasin moves to his theme, which is that, 'We have abandoned our historical masterpieces – with their Greek columns, Gothic ornaments, yellow-stoned arches and Seljuk-ian domes – to destruction and pillage.' Discussing the ruin of the Kyrenia district, he writes:

> There you will see small churches which have suffered the fate of the Armenian monastery in Halevga and of other churches. You will ask, well, where is that old Omer Tekke? It used to stand on the sea like a water lily before 1974. Now it has become a withered flower with its crude wall plasters, with its destroyed marble fountain abandoned to nature's destructive forces. Do not ask any questions about the condition of the first-century city of Lamboussa, which is now a military zone.

Adds Yasin,

> Be careful, do not expose the grief of your heart to the Kyrenians, because they will tell you even worse things. They will explain how Kyrenia castle was robbed – actually, hasn't the whole of Kyrenia been stolen? If you sit at a coffee-shop you will observe that the Limassoleans in Kyrenia constantly express their longing for Limassol. But what will you say when you see that even the Kyrenians long for Kyrenia? – I think this is the most agonizing longing.

Yasin makes it clear that religious bigotry as well as greed is at work here. He describes the 'hysteric obliteration' in Morphou, where 'a concrete mosque has been erected in front of the Byzantine church of St Mamas, which is adorned with Gothic arches'. Then he gives more detail:

> Haven't you heard that the 2,000-year-old Christian church in Cyprus, St Barnabas's Church, has been robbed? Haven't

you heard that thirty-five icons were stolen, that eleven of them were found in Kythrea, that eleven were retrieved at Ankara airport while being smuggled out, and that the rest are lost?

Haven't you heard what's happening in Varosha (Famagusta)? Haven't you heard that figurines belonging to the Catholic period and kept in the Archaeological Museum have been stolen and smuggled to London?

What about the icons in the other churches; the mosaics, the private collections, the illegal digs? Haven't you heard of these? Why have they stopped the digs started before 1974 at the city of Gastria, which belongs to the Geometric age? Do you know what has happened since then? The government has issued permits to certain businessmen from Turkey to set up a gypsum factory there. The tombs were destroyed and plundered.

The Turkish archaeologist Dr Turhan Kamil takes up Yasin's story. He describes how both the ancient city sites of 'Salamis and Engomi are completely abandoned. In my latest research I noticed that the wire fencing Salamis had been stolen. No serious work is being done in Engomi.'

Though he writes with some circumspection, and confines himself as far as possible to the battle to save the antiquities of Cyprus, Mehmet Yasin makes it clear that three strong forces really control the destiny of the Turkish Cypriots. These are Mr Rauf Denktash's National Unity Party (NUP), the Turkish army and the Islamic religious foundation Evkaf. This is interesting, because these are the three forces that more than any other have obstructed a negotiated settlement in Cyprus and have devoted themselves to making the north of the island into a *de facto* province of Turkey. Yasin, then, has described a microcosm of the colonization which is apparent at the political and the international levels.

As he says in describing the ancient city of Lamboussa, a city with an immense past in the Roman and Byzantine periods:

You will see chambers cut out of the rocks, lighthouses, the remains of baths, mosaic lay-outs and the military camps set up on the ruins both before and after 1974. Today Lamboussa is a military zone closed to tourists. Here there are many important churches and the mythological Akhiropietos Monastery. Now you cannot see it because it is being used as a military warehouse.

Lamboussa has that in common with other areas of Cyprus, including the city of Varosha and the area of Apostolos Andreas. These are off limits even to Turkish Cypriots. No Turkish Cypriot official is empowered to authorize a visit there, even for a visiting foreign journalist or specialist. The real power in the north is held by the Turkish army and its allies.

Among the latter, the most prominent is Mr Rauf Denktash's National Unity Party. Ever since the days of the TMT underground, this faction has expressed the ambitions of conservative Turkish nationalism in Cyprus. Dr Kuchuk, again writing in his daily *Halkin Sesi*, confirms that from 1957 he was in touch with Riza Vuruskan, the Turkish officer who led and founded TMT; first to help the British and then to fight against the Greeks and the Turkish Cypriot radicals. Dr Kuchuk recalled, on Vuruskan's death in 1979, that in the 1950s he

used to go to Ankara very frequently. During one of these visits, the late Prime Minister of Turkey, Adnan Menderes, introduced Riza Vuruskan to me . . . Later on I met him at the office of a lieutenant general and talked with him there. During our meeting it was decided that Vuruskan should come to Cyprus as 'civilian adviser'. He arrived in Cyprus under an assumed name.

Mr Denktash has also given his reminiscences of that period, in which he admitted for the first time what had long been suspected – that he had been among the founders of TMT:

Everybody thought I was the leader but I was not. I was political adviser. Immediately after forming it I handed it over. It was a good mask because even the British and American intelligence thought I was the man who decided everything. I was not. The leaders were former army officers from Turkey. [*The Times*, 20 January 1978]

In Turkish political terms, before the abolition of independent parties, the NUP would have straddled the right wing of the conservative Justice Party, with room at its extremity for supporters of the Fascist National Action Party of Colonel Turkes. Through forces like the Idealist Hearth Associations, exact duplicates of those on the mainland and known under the same name of Ulku Ocaklari, the NUP is able to remind dissenters of the reserve strength possessed by the old TMT.

In interviews with Turkish Cypriot political leaders, I have been able to form some impression of the nature of Mr Denktash's regime. It is described by the main opposition leader, Mr Alpay Durduran of the Communal Liberation Party, as 'a Rightist movement with Fascist tendencies'. The leader of the more radical Republican Turkish Party, Mr Osker Ozgur, agrees with this characterization and stresses that Mr Denktash is a client of the Turkish military. He told me that on 21 August 1981, when elections had left Mr Denktash's party without a dependable majority (despite its resources as the governing party and despite its hidden support from mainland settler voters) there was a meeting to discuss a coalition government. Mr Ilter Turkmen, then the Turkish junta's Foreign Minister, was present at the meeting and told Mr Ozgur personally that his party would not be allowed into a coalition because of its criticisms of NATO. As a result of this direct interference from Ankara, Mr Denktash's party survived its electoral reverses at the hands of disgruntled Turkish Cypriots. Both Mr Durduran and Mr Ozgur are opposed to partition. But they will both admit, ruefully, that their relatively large electoral following is not primarily due to their stand on the national question. It comes from the strong popular resentment about the division of the spoils. In Dr Kuchuk's *Halkin Sesi* again, there has been constant criticism of this state of affairs. One editorial complained that, 'only a handful of people have become rich by plundering and stealing; the majority of the Turkish Cypriots are low-income people. . . Today there is a rich class in the Turkish Cypriot community created by the government for its own ends.' Life in the north is dominated by those who operate concessions with Turkey and who have the right contacts in the *nouveau riche* occupation establishment. This can decide anything from an import licence to a permission to operate a confiscated Greek hotel. It can also decide positions of political influence. Mr Nejat Konuk, the first Prime Minister of the 'Turkish Federated State of Kibris' and Mr Osman Orek, the first president of its assembly, both departed from Mr Denktash's party in protest at this kind of exorbitance and parasitism.* Other political leaders have issued strong criticisms of the economic 'Caesars' who form the new class. Clearly, since the economy of the 'state' is a function of Turkey, and since the only legal currency is the Turkish lira, it is businessmen connected with the motherland who stand the best chance. Thus when Mehmet Yasin writes about the horrible desecration of the Geometric city of Gastria, he mentions quite naturally that the gypsum and cement factory, run by mainland Turks, was erected on the site because, 'the mouthpiece and partners of the two Turkish Republic citizens, Fevzi Akkaya and Sezai Turkes, who own the cement factory, are NUP people'.

The third important presence mentioned by Mehmet Yasin is that of Evkaf, the Islamic religious trust. He notes the indifference of Evkaf to any cultural or environmental or historic consideration, unless that consideration bears upon mosques in active present-day use. Evkaf's role is not well understood by many Turkish Cypriots, who are secular in their everyday habits, but it has been known to play an important part in events. In 1979, for example, when it was proposed that the return of the empty city of Varosha (Famagusta) to the Greek Cypriots could open a settlement negotiation, the whole discussion was thrown awry by Evkaf's insistence that all of Famagusta (including the Greek-owned houses and businesses modestly estimated by Yasin at sixty per cent) was legally Turkish. This claim, founded on untenable Ottoman imperial precedents, was not pursued after it had had the desired effect

* Immediately after his 'UDI' in November 1983, Mr Denktash rewrote his own constitution, increasing the forty-member assembly by thirty seats. Most of the new members are personal nominees. This measure was taken without the supposedly obligatory two-thirds majority or popular referendum.

of negating the talks. The mainland Turkish daily *Aydinlik* (*Clarity*), a radical paper admired by its rivals and since closed by the Turkish army for good, commented scornfully that: 'One wonders to which Pashas Athens, Salonika, Belgrade and Budapest belong. If they also belong to Pashas, then we could soon reach the gates of Vienna again.'

On other occasions, Mr Denktash and his allies have found it convenient to invoke Islam. They have done so selectively, usually in order to gain or woo support from the Arab world – which has so far been unimpressed. There was even, in 1979, an opportunistic flirtation with the idea of declaring northern Cyprus an Islamic republic. The scheme came to nothing. For one thing it would logically have necessitated the removal of all the busts and plaques of the great secularist Kemal Atatürk, mass-produced and mass-installed across the island since 1974. Even without this embarrassment, there would have been political difficulties. Turkey is too closely linked to Israel, and its imperial hegemony over the Arab world is too well remembered, for it now to pose as the champion of the oppressed faithful.

Turkish Cypriots are very defensive about their 'state'. They tend to keep quarrels and complaints within the family, to publish them only in Turkish, and to answer all objections and criticisms with a recitation of their past woes at the hands of the Greeks. This makes Mehmet Yasin's testimony the more impressive. I have read many laments by Greeks for the world they have lost, and for the ruin of their beloved island home. Few are as affecting as Yasin's from 'the other side'.

Attila is quite a common first name in Turkey. It is also well-known in western Europe, with the difference that there it is a name used to frighten children. The code-name 'Attila' was given at one stage to the Turkish army's move on Cyprus. The name stuck long after the code-name had been superseded. One can see why. Such a titanic failure in public relations was, from the Greek point of view, irresistible. It summoned every image of pitiless barbarism, and evoked every memory of the Asiatic hordes. Precisely for that reason, it is almost valueless as a metaphor for the 1974 invasion. That invasion, as I hope to have shown, was not a medieval or fanatical blood-feast. It was conducted, and is sustained, with the help of men whose habitat is air-conditioned and whose style is sophisticated. It was a thoroughly modern and political attempt to amputate the Republic of Cyprus. The weapons used were twentieth-century, and so were the methods.

The powers of the modern, advanced world accepted the dismemberment of Cyprus when they did not actually collude with it. Nevertheless, the events of the summer of 1974 were disturbing to political life in many countries. There had to be an accounting, which in four capitals was very educational.

V Consequences

Washington

Cyprus provided the occasion for a battle between the United States Congress and the Executive which continues to this day. If, now, an American President feels constrained in what he may do overseas without congressional consent, then it is the unfortunate Cypriots who can take a large share of the credit.

One says a large share because although Cyprus was the ostensible occasion for the conflict, it was one which had too long been postponed. By the summer of 1974, many senior senators and Congressmen were fed up with learning, after the fact, that the United States had been responsible for some discreditable foreign imbroglio. There had been the secret bombing of Cambodia, and the endless manifestations of Richard Nixon's double-dealing over Vietnam. There had been the awful massacre, with American weapons, of insurgent Bangladesh. There had been the engineering of a military coup in Chile. Now there was a near-war in NATO and the other bitter consequences of an obviously rank intimacy with the Greek junta. Congress was, quite simply, tired of being kept in the dark. And the new favourite policy – backing of Turkey – did not look any more appetizing.

On 15 August, as the Turkish army was planting its flag on the partition line and driving tens of thousands of Greek Cypriots into exile in their own country, a delegation of Congressmen called on Kissinger to demand an embargo on arms to Turkey; arms which had been supplied on the strict understanding that they were to be used to defend Turkey

against the Soviet Union. The delegation was led by Congressman John Brademas, a Greek American from Indiana.
Brademas was not impressed by Kissinger's argument that the
United States was pursuing 'very active diplomacy' with the
Turkish government. Assurances, so easily offered and so
quickly forgotten, and so glibly packaged with a plea that
Congress should not 'tie the hands' of the Executive, were no
longer enough. Laurence Stern of the *Washington Post*, in his
excellent book *The Wrong Horse*, describes the substance of the
meeting at the State Department:

> The Indiana Democrat [Brademas] pronounced Kissinger's
> efforts at private diplomacy a failure. He asked why there
> had been no public protest from the State Department when
> Makarios was overthrown and nearly murdered, or when the
> Turks had invaded Cyprus. Why, he went on, were there no
> public statements of support for Callaghan in his efforts to
> keep the Turks from leaving the bargaining table at Geneva?
> Why was the State Department virtually silent during the
> ensuing military blitz by Turkish troops?

These were all, except the third, which was too philanthropic
towards Callaghan, good questions. And to none of them did
Kissinger have a convincing answer. His strategy, in the coming
weeks and months, was to refer disparagingly to his critics as
'the Greek lobby' – as if they were motivated by purely ethnic
concerns and were somehow diminished thereby. This
approach had two weaknesses. The first was that the description did not cover Senator Claiborne Pell, Senator Vance
Hartke, Congressman Don Fraser or Congressman Benjamin
Rosenthal, to name only some of the prominent politicians who
supported Brademas's effort. The second was that Dr Kissinger
himself had been a political ally of Spiro Agnew and Thomas
Pappas, both of whom had formed a 'Greek lobby' on behalf of
the junta.
    The lack of understanding on this point went as far as the
White House. When Congressman Brademas called on President Ford shortly after he took office, and again patiently
explained his objections to the use of American arms for

Turkish expansionism, he was met by the astounding presidential interjection that, 'After all, it was the Greeks who started this thing.' It had, indeed, been 'the Greeks' who started 'this thing'. But the Greeks in question were a minority enjoying the support of Nixon, Kissinger and Ford. Brademas, who had opposed the junta, did not feel bound by its legacy. It was becoming apparent that there had been a 'double tilt', first in favour of Greece for as long as it was a dictatorship, and then away from Greece and Cyprus and towards Turkey when the Athens government returned to democracy. A democratic regime was now to be punished for the not wholly involuntary crimes of an authoritarian one. This rather crude policy was a counterpart abroad to the administration's distrust of democracy in foreign policy-making at home. It had the effect of enhancing congressional determination to recover at least some control over America's overseas commitments. There was almost nothing that Kissinger would not do to prevent this outcome. His implied view, that democracy and an effective foreign policy were somehow incompatible, became less implied and more explicit as the debate gathered momentum. Cyprus may have looked like 'a flea' to him as it had to his predecessors. But there must have been times, in the ensuing months, when he regretted swatting at it so callously.

Kissinger has, throughout his career, regarded the law as a rough guide. His irritation at its exactitude or its codification is notorious. Cyprus was, for him, an unwelcome test case of a precisely worded law – the Foreign Assistance Act. Under the terms of the FAA, which was promulgated in 1961, a nation became 'immediately ineligible for further assistance' if it used American weapons in 'substantial violation' of the act's restrictions. The FAA also enjoined the President to deny aid to 'any country which is engaging in or preparing for aggressive military efforts directed against any country receiving assistance under this or any other act'. Cyprus, as the recipient of several American aid programmes, qualified for that protection, just as Turkey qualified for that denial.

The high ground of the Foreign Assistance Act was not undermined by either of the two other relevant diplomatic agreements. These were the bilateral agreements of 1947 between the United States and Turkey, which forbade the diversion of American weapons to any other country without the prior consent of the President, and the 1960 London–Zurich agreements which excluded partition in name and in fact. It would be understating the legal position to say that the United States had little choice but to place an embargo on further arms shipments to Turkey. Its own laws required that it do so.

For this reason, Kissinger did not enter any legal challenge to his critics. He preferred to shroud himself in the same discredited 'executive privilege' which had postponed the resignation of his patron Richard Nixon. He professed ignorance of the law from the first, as on the famous occasion when he was asked, on 19 August 1974, whether the Foreign Assistance Act did not necessitate the termination of aid to Turkey. His reply was: 'Well, I will have to get a legal opinion on that, which I have not done.'

Turkish troops had been taking village after village in Cyprus for over a month when the self-anointed king of foreign policy gave that reply. Meanwhile, State Department legal officers were set to work, but by September had concluded that there was no lawful basis for continued military aid to Turkey. The finding of the law officers was, however, not acted upon. Instead, Congress was asked to consider Turkey's special position as a NATO ally with 1,000 miles of border with the Soviet Union. Gone was the insistence on the importance of (junta) Greece as a 'home port' for the Sixth Fleet. Now, Turkey was the prize and the most favoured nation. So transparent was the opportunism of this argument that many important Republican votes went to make up the Senate's resolution, by sixty-four votes to twenty-seven, for an embargo. The administration's logic was circular. It alleged that Turkey might default on its NATO obligations if it was threatened with Congressional pressure, but it omitted to say that by directing troops, planes and weapons to Cyprus, Turkey had already weakened its NATO commitment. The administration further alleged that political isolation of Turkey was 'counter-productive', an exhausted neologism and one that, given the stand of Ford and Kissinger, was self-fulfilling. If the Turks knew that the White House and the Defense Department were opposed to congressional sanctions, they had only to wait, as the Greek junta had done, for a change in policy. By the logic of Dr Kissinger, Turkey's refusal to make any concessions on Cyprus was a *vindication* of his policy and a rebuke to congressional resolve. His own position in the argument was, however, very far from neutral. And his hypocritical view that Turkey would respond to generosity rather than an embargo was soon disproved. In late 1975 the embargo was partially lifted after a very narrow vote in Congress, and after a series of public and private 'assurances' from Ankara about concessions. No concession has been made since. It is fair to conclude, then, that the pride of Turkey was affronted by the embargo experiment, but that its real determination was not tested. Divided between administration 'realism' and congressional 'idealism', American policy once again achieved the worst of both worlds.

Cyprus was to American foreign policy the counterpart, in timing and in character, of Watergate in domestic policy. Like Watergate, it ended in a stalemate, with the principal villains discredited but unpunished. Like Watergate, it gave Congress and the press a brief opportunity to subject policy-making to critical scrutiny. But the sense of outrage generated by the scrutiny was, as in the case of Watergate, not to prove durable. By the time that Presidents Nixon and Ford, and their executor Dr Kissinger, had been replaced, the United States was back to business as usual with Turkey.

I do not make the Watergate comparison solely for effect. There was a strong, continuous relationship between the upper reaches of the Nixon team and the Greek junta. Much of this relationship remained uninvestigated, or partially investigated, when the various Watergate committees had completed their formal tasks. The number of unresolved questions was skilfully defined by Senator George McGovern, Nixon's defrauded opponent in the 1972 presidential election, and chairman of the Senate Subcommittee on Near Eastern and South Asian Affairs. On 29 October 1976 he wrote a letter to Senator Daniel Inouye, the chairman of the Senate Select Committee on Intelligence. The letter, which has lost none of its relevance, came into my possession in 1983. I reproduce it here in full:

Dear Mr Chairman,
As chairman of the Senate Subcommittee on Near Eastern
and South Asian Affairs, and as a member of the Committee
on Foreign Relations, I have closely followed American
foreign policy interests in Greece during the military
dictatorship there, during the restoration of democracy after
the 1974 Cyprus coup, and in connection with the involvement of our intelligence agencies with Greece during both
periods. I write to bring to your attention information
concerning Greece and our intelligence agencies which
merit, I am convinced, a careful investigation by your
committee. Because this information covers events over the
past eight years both in Greece and this country, and because
many individuals, both Greek and American, are involved, I
have summarized the data below:

I. *Unresolved Questions from Senate Intelligence Investigation*
The Church Committee's case study of covert action in
Greece, as long as it remains secret, cannot be assessed for
its consideration of the involvement of intelligence agencies
in the 1967 coup against the democratic government in
Greece, in the 1974 coup against President Makarios of
Cyprus or in efforts to use CIA facilities or funds for
domestic political purposes. Secretary of State Kissinger,
former CIA director William Colby and former special CIA
counsel Mitchell Rogovin are all quoted by responsible
journalists as stating that our covert involvement in Greece
was substantial enough to endanger our present (i.e.,
post-Watergate and post-1974) relations with the democratic
government of Greece.

II. *The Role of Former Vice President Agnew in the 1968
Presidential Campaign Concerning Greece*
Mr Agnew offered to testify in summer 1975 before the
Church Committee on charges that he changed his position
from one of 'neutrality' toward the Greek military dictatorship in 1968 to support for the junta. The reason for this
change in Agnew's view has never been investigated. The
Greek government ended plans for its own study of whether
the military junta's intelligence arm, KYP, which was closely

associated with and financed by the CIA, funneled secret funds back to the United States for use in the 1968 presidential campaign. The Greek government's decision not to pursue this investigation came at the request of the CIA station chief in Athens. The present suspicion that CIA funds and 'fronts' were involved in either the 1968 American election or in the Watergate cover-up should be dispelled by a thorough investigation.

III. *Efforts Directed Against Elias Demetracopoulos*

Demetracopoulos came to the United States in late 1967 in self-imposed exile from the military dictatorship which had taken over in Athens earlier that year. During the 1967–74 period he waged a continuous battle against the Greek junta and against US policies supporting the dictators. He incurred the animosity of both the Greek and the American governments. In Washington, he was threatened with deportation by Attorney-General John Mitchell, denounced in an anonymous State Department memorandum, his Wall Street employers were visited by FBI agents, the congressional committee before which he testified was visited by a Justice Department agent, and slanderous raw material and disinformation from CIA operatives about Demetracopoulos was given to reporters and freelance writers like Russell Howe and Sarah Trott. In Greece, Demetracopoulos was deprived of his citizenship and refused entry to the country even for a brief visit to attend his father's funeral. There are also reports that the KYP, aided by CIA, planned to kidnap Demetracopoulos and return him to Greece to end his Washington anti-junta efforts and to interrogate him. These efforts, in so far as they originated in or were aided by US government agencies, deserve a full and careful examination.

IV. *The Role of Thomas Pappas*

Pappas, who commutes between Boston and Athens, is a prosperous Greek–American businessman with dual nationality who has been a major fund-raiser for both President Nixon and President Ford. Pappas also maintained close ties with the Greek junta during its seven-year reign. Both his Athens and his Washington connections were based on a skilful combination of business and political connections which served Pappas's considerable investments in Greece as well as his role as a conduit between the two governments. Pappas was the subject of a memorandum presented to a House subcommittee investigating US policies toward the Greek junta. Shortly after this memorandum was submitted by its author, Elias Demetracopoulos, he was threatened with deportation (see III above) by Attorney-General John Mitchell and by President Nixon's close associate, Murray Chotiner. Pappas was the first person named by President Nixon in the White House tapes as the man to be approached for money to satisfy the demands of Watergate burglar E. Howard Hunt. Pappas is involved as both a fund-raiser and contributor to the Ford campaign, and he is a member of President Ford's Finance Committee. He served President Nixon in similar roles. The extensive and longstanding ties of Pappas to the Greek junta, to domestic US policies and the intelligence community, and the use of Greek and US intelligence agencies (which worked together on many matters) to question in turn those who questioned these Pappas roles indicates a need for a thorough investigation of his activities by your committee to the extent it can be established that these activities involved our intelligence agencies.

The above summaries outline some of the major areas involving Greece and the intelligence community which deserve a more complete and public examination than was provided in the limited time available to your predecessor committee.

Attached you will find material relating to the above points which you may find of interest.

I will be happy to furnish additional details on the matters outlined above which I trust are presented in sufficient detail to indicate both the complexity and serious nature of the charges involved.

Sincerely,
George McGovern

Subsequent correspondence between the two senators, including a letter also in my possession dated 7 June 1977, shows that Senator McGovern was invited to view the Intelligence Committee's report on Greece and related subjects, but in confidence and without the presence of aides or of *aides-memoires*. He quite properly declined, preferring to request that the report be made public. The argument against this was, once again, that it would damage and compromise relations with conservative forces in Greece.

Later evidence shows that McGovern was asking the right questions. In 1976 the House Intelligence Committee took sworn but off-the-record evidence from Henry Tasca, Nixon's ambassador to Greece. Tasca confirmed that the Greek junta had indeed made campaign contributions to the Nixon–Agnew election fund. As Seymour Hersh relates in his book, *The Price of Power: Kissinger in the Nixon White House*:

In 1972, Pappas served as a principal Nixon fund-raiser and as a vice president of the finance committee of the Committee to Re-Elect the President. It was not until 1976, however, that the House Intelligence Committee was able to confirm Demetracopoulos's allegations against Pappas. It received sworn evidence from Henry J. Tasca, a career Foreign Service officer who had been Nixon's ambassador to Greece, that in 1968 Pappas had served as a conduit for campaign funds from the Greek government to the Nixon campaign. Tasca's statement was made off the record – at his insistence, according to a committee investigator – and was not published. . .

Tasca's information about the junta's campaign contributions to the 1968 Nixon election campaign raises the question whether the CIA, which was financing the Greek intelligence operations at the same time, was aware that some of its funds were being returned to the United States for use in the presidential election. This question was not looked into by the Senate Intelligence Committee during its CIA inquiries in 1975 and 1976. Sources close to the committee have said that its investigation was abruptly cancelled at Kissinger's direct request. He urged the committee to drop the investigation, one official said, on the ground that relations between the United States and Greece would be 'severely harmed'.*

Kissinger's motives were, of course, quite different. 'Severe harm' would have been done, rather, to relations between himself and his political masters, as well as to relations between himself and a generally sycophantic press. The fact that Thomas Pappas was the link between the junta and the Nixon camp, the fact that Laurence O'Brien, chairman of the Democratic Party, had called for a public investigation of those links, the fact that it was Laurence O'Brien's office that the Watergate burglars had 'targeted', and the fact that it was Thomas Pappas who was approached by the Nixon White House to pay the burglars' 'hush money' (Pappas having been vice chairman of the finance committee of the Committee to Re-Elect the President) *may* all be quite unconnected. But those facts are authenticated, and they show how the same gangster principles were at work in the foreign policy of the Nixon White House as were unearthed in its domestic policy. Cyprus was the victim of those who behaved as if the American administration was their private property.

Athens

Dr Kissinger was right about one thing. Disclosures about Cyprus and the junta did continue to jeopardize the restoration of conservative democracy in Athens.

The new government of Constantine Karamanlis was anxious to retain and rebuild good relations with the United States, along the lines of the cold-war consensus that had existed in the 1950s and 1960s. But it had also to deal with an aroused public opinion, which was furious at American collusion with the junta and American favouritism towards Turkey. In this rather

---

*Pappas appears in the White House tapes of 26 April 1973. John Haldeman, in the presence of Nixon, quotes John Dean as talking to Attorney-General John Mitchell about hush money for the burglars. 'Dean says, "Did you talk to the Greek?" Mitchell said, "Yes, I have." Dean says, "Is the Greek bearing gifts?" Mitchell said, "Well, I'm gonna call you tomorrow on that."'

testing situation, where identification with United States interests had become a heavy political liability, the issue of Cyprus became crucial.

In modern Greek history, there is a close relationship between national humiliation and political radicalization. The defeat of Greek armies by Kemal Ataturk in Asia Minor in 1922 led to a purge of the officer corps, widespread distrust of the Establishment, the enforced exile of the royal family, and the influx of hundreds of thousands of refugees who formed a new proletariat and contributed to the rise of Marxist and workers' parties throughout the 1930s. The subjugation of Greece by the Axis powers in 1941, which had been preceded by a local Fascist dictatorship under General Metaxas, led not just to a national resistance but to an internal class war and a serious attempt by the Greek Communist Party to convert the war of liberation into a victory for Josef Stalin. (Stalin turned out not to be interested, having privately 'swapped' Greece for Rumania and Bulgaria at pre-Yalta discussions with Winston Churchill.) Throughout the conservative decades that followed, it was on the issue of Cyprus that the semi-legal Leftist parties were able to have an impact beyond their own constituency. Here were Greek-speaking people being sacrificed to British interests and to NATO, and what did the 'patriotic' governments propose to do about it? It was this criticism, and others like it, which put Greek conservative politicians like Karamanlis and Averoff on the spot before the London–Zurich agreements of 1960. After the terrible events of 1974 this rhetoric acquired renewed force. The junta had draped itself in the Greek flag, in Greek Orthodoxy, in so-called 'Hellenic' values, and yet had sold out Cyprus to the dictates of Henry Kissinger – thereby in effect abandoning it to the Turks. So ran a large current of demotic opinion.

After Constantine Karamanlis returned to Athens and even before he had won a decisive victory with his hurriedly formed New Democracy party, Greece withdrew from the military, but not the political, wing of NATO. This was in protest at the Turkish occupation of Cyprus which was tolerated, to say the least, by Dr Joseph Luns, NATO's then Secretary-General, and by most of the members of the alliance. The withdrawal was

also intended to appease anti-NATO sentiment among the
Greek voters. For Karamanlis, the great anti-Communist
statesman of the 1950s and 1960s, this was no small step. But
the other half of his balancing act was just as important if rather
less public. It consisted of a strenuous effort to restore friendly
relations with Washington. The 'two-track' policy might well
have succeeded if the United States had shown any interest in
disciplining Turkey or in reunifying Cyprus. Instead, the
Ford–Kissinger administration continued its romance with
Ankara. It made an inept attempt, using the primate of the
Greek American community, Archbishop Iakovos, to placate
Greek–American feeling. But this effort was fruitless except in
demonstrating to a wide public that Karamanlis was desperate
for concessions.

At a meeting in the White House on 7 October 1974,
Archbishop Iakovos met Ford and Kissinger and asked them
for some sign of Turkish concessions to help, 'in pacifying my
flock'. According to Iakovos, Kissinger replied that the Greek
Prime Minister and Foreign Minister, 'Messrs Mavros and
Karamanlis, do not want us to make any announcement before
the elections . . . obviously, they are afraid of being accused as
friends of America and then there is fear of losing the elections.
I do repeat,' said Kissinger, 'that we want to help Greece and
particularly Mr Karamanlis because the movement around
[Andreas] Papandreou is strong and disturbing. We do not wish
at all to see Papandreou governing Greece.' Archbishop
Iakovos, a theological and political conservative, recorded in
his memorandum of the meeting that, 'the President was
sincere and cordial. I am sorry but I cannot say the same for Mr
Kissinger'. The leaking of that memorandum, in Greece and in
the USA, came too late to forestall Karamanlis's election
victory in November of that year. But it did give point to the
criticisms levelled by Andreas Papandreou that the Greek
Right was lukewarm about Cyprus and hypocritical in its
criticisms of Kissinger.

In a fierce debate on foreign policy in the Greek Parliament
on 16 October 1975, George Mavros denounced the Iakovos
memorandum, from the Right, as a piece of CIA disinformation. He accused Andreas Papandreou of profiting by the

spreading of such falsehoods. Once the document had been confirmed as authentic by the Archbishop and by congressional sources, Mavros was forced to withdraw these accusations against Papandreou and against the man who had furnished the document, Elias Demetracopoulos. He went so far as to say, in an interview with the newspaper *Athinaiki*, that the Iakovos memorandum was 'the most important political event in Greece in the last twenty years'. Again, he was guilty of an exaggeration. But the controversy over the memorandum was decisive in making Papandreou, rather than Mavros, the leader of the main opposition in Greece and the axiomatic challenger for the post of Prime Minister.

In March 1976 the Ford administration rewarded the patience of its Greek allies by signing a new base agreement with Turkey. The Greek reaction was to insist unsuccessfully on equal treatment with Turkey in matters military – a nervous response which made it clear that Athens cared more about good relations with Washington than it did about Cyprus, but could achieve progress with neither. The arms embargo, meanwhile, was being diluted to the point where it would obviously be repealed soon. In these circumstances, Turkey felt offended rather than hampered. And the Greek government opted to cut its losses, by ceasing to press for the embargo's continuation. From one perspective, it is hard to blame Karamanlis for doing this. But the obvious *realpolitik* of his approach only lent weight to Andreas Papandreou's increasingly successful opposition movement PASOK. The initials stood for Pan-Hellenic Socialist Movement, and they symbolized the energetic way in which Papandreou, accused of unpatriotic Leftism in the sixties, had synthesized national feeling with radical political ideas. This, given Papandreou's long association with Cyprus, was no coincidence. His new party had as one of its chief slogans the demand to 'open the Cyprus file'. The demand expressed the popular view that there should be a public trial for those responsible for the 1974 disaster, just as there had been of the junta's torturers. There was probably no actual 'Cyprus file', but the responsibility for the coup against Makarios went inconveniently high, and was a continual source of embarrassment to a centre-Right government anxious for the loyalty of its officer corps.

Hopes were briefly aroused by the election of Jimmy Carter as President of the United States. The government of Cyprus declared a public holiday (as much for the departure of Henry Kissinger as for the accession of the Georgian). The new President swiftly disappointed his Greek allies – as he was to disappoint all those who reposed their confidence in him. In spite of a campaign promise to the contrary, he asked Congress to repeal the arms embargo on Turkey completely, and by September 1978 he had succeeded in convincing them. The policy worked as smoothly as it did because Carter's congressional allies attached a $35 million grant aid provision for Greece. They were greatly assisted by a letter from Karamanlis to Carter, which set out in advance what Greece's conditions were. They were three: no linkage between aid to Greece and progress on Cyprus; a preservation of the military balance in the eastern Mediterranean; peace in the region after repeal of the embargo. As the indefatigable Elias Demetracopoulos wrote to former Senator Frank Moss, 'these priorities of Karamanlis were thus known to the White House *before* the crucial House vote. The White House lobbyists used that knowledge of Karamanlis's real interests in helping to persuade House members that Greece did not really oppose repeal.'

The end of the embargo saw the end of any Turkish pretence at concessions on Cyprus. It also put Greece in a somewhat false position *vis-à-vis* NATO and the United States. The Turkish government, ungrateful for its tacit support for repeal, continued to oppose the readmission of Greece to the NATO command. And this, in turn, made Karamanlis (and his successor George Rallis) more openly dependent on American support. This, too, gave ammunition to Andreas Papandreou. It was all very well to be close to Washington if it led to results. But Cyprus had been abandoned and the military and economic alliance between the United States and Turkey was getting stronger all the time. In November 1981, Papandreou and his party gained an unexpectedly large victory in the Greek elections, putting an end to almost half a century of uninterrupted conservative rule. There can be little doubt that it was the Cyprus issue, in its various dimensions, which made this outcome possible. It was ambitions over Cyprus which helped the junta to power. It was Cyprus which helped to sustain it in power and to guarantee it American support. It was Cyprus which brought the junta down. And it was Cyprus which, by discrediting the Greek Establishment so widely, created the decisive opening to the Left. By 1981 George Mavros, who had been Deputy Premier and Foreign Minister in the first Karamanlis government of 1974, was calling on his centrist supporters to vote for PASOK, which many of them did.

Andreas Papandreou, immediately upon taking office, set a more forward position on the Cyprus question. He became the first Greek Prime Minister to pay a visit to the island. He defined its problem as one of invasion and occupation rather than as one of intercommunal relations. He offered Greek financing for a larger United Nations peacekeeping force on condition that the Turkish army left. He virtually declared that Greece would regard any further attack on Cyprus as an attack on itself. These initiatives, combined with greater tension in the Aegean, a rapidly mounting regional arms race, and the unilateral Turkish 'declaration of independence' of 15 November 1983, combined to put Cyprus much higher on the international register of concern than it had been since 1974.

Many mainland Greeks are now exhausted by the Cyprus issue. It has gone on for too long, and has provided too many occasions for domestic destabilization and external danger. It could yet be the site of another Graeco–Turkish war. It absorbs a great deal of Greek aid. Yet, in spite of all these unwelcome considerations, it is impossible for Greece to 'drop' Cyprus. The island represents the past: Turkish domination of the Greek world. It represents the present: the worst of the many bad hangovers from the junta period. In a fashion, also, it represents the future. Cyprus is emblematic of all the difficulties faced by an emerging modern Greece, which seeks to escape from being a Balkan country dependent on America, and to become a respected member of the European community. The greatest obstacle to that evolution is the costly and ancient rivalry with Turkey. The greatest impediment to resolution of that conflict is Cyprus.

London

The aftermath of the Cyprus crisis had an unexpected result in the United Kingdom as well. It led to a brief but glorious moment of open government. For the first time, a Select Committee of the House of Commons acted like an American Congressional Committee and questioned senior members of the Executive and the Legislative branches in public. The Cyprus Select Committee carried out as thorough an investigation as any House of Commons Committee ever had, despite being refused access to the occupied north of the island.

The Foreign Secretary, James Callaghan, grudgingly appeared before the all-party group on 19 February 1976, and made a spectacular fool of himself. Under questioning from both Conservative and Labour MPs, Mr Callaghan decided on the stonewall tactic of pleading ignorance, a tactic to which his general demeanour lent tone but not credibility. It was, perhaps, less costly to appear stupid than it would have been to admit to knowledge. Still, the Foreign Secretary took his doggedness a little far. I watched, fascinated, his 'know-nothing' performance. Flanked by three advisers, Messrs Goodison, Burden and Freeland, Mr Callaghan took up position.

Questioned on whether he still recognized the original Treaty of Guarantee: 'I do not know the law as clearly as some.'

On whether he had made preparations with the Ministry of Defence before the Turkish invasion: 'I do not know what you are referring to.'

On anticipating the invasion: 'Nobody knew where the invasion was likely to come from, whether from Greece or Turkey.'

On reports of Turkish troop movements which he had received at the Geneva talks: 'Was that right?' (turning to his aide Mr Goodison).

On whether the British forces in the north of Cyprus could have been deployed in a different way: 'I suppose so. I do not know.'

On whether there were enough British forces to have secured the northern coast: 'I am not able to comment on that because I just do not know at this stage.'

On whether there had been direct discussions between Greek and Turkish Cypriots on bi-zonal federation: 'I do not remember.' (Mr Goodison took over.)

On whether Archbishop Makarios had accepted the three-point settlement or not: 'I think you are going beyond my knowledge.' (Mr Goodison took over.)

On whether British citizens had been assured of British government protection in the event of war, and if he understood the relevant clause in the treaty: 'I am sorry, where is that. . . I can only repeat this parrot-wise, but I am told this has nothing to do with the Treaty of Guarantee.'

On whether the Turkish government had changed its mind on compensation: (Mr Burden had to answer for him).

On whether the Foreign Office in 1974 had advised British residents not to return to their homes: 'When was this advice given, could you tell me?' Told that it was in October 1974, by the Consular Emergency Unit of the Foreign Office: 'What did it say?'

On the status of the refugees within the British 'sovereign base' areas: 'I doubt if I can answer that. Mr Goodison had better try.'

On whether the High Commissioner had a hardship fund: 'I am afraid I am not aware of that.'

The chairman of the Select Committee asked Callaghan whether he could say if he had any advance intelligence of the 15 July Sampson coup. He replied, 'No.' He was then asked, 'You mean you cannot say?' He replied, 'No, there was no advance intelligence.' Pressed on this point, he gave it as his considered opinion that nobody knew of the impending coup except the Greek junta and its Cypriot mercenaries. This, as we now know, was not the truth.

After Callaghan's appalling performance, the committee's report to the House of Commons only just managed to remain within the confines of parliamentary language. It concluded drily that, 'the Foreign Secretary's evidence was confusing. . . Your committee find it difficult to accept that all three stages of the crisis came as a surprise to the Government.' This laconic understatement encapsulated one of the deadliest works of criticism ever published by Her Majesty's Stationery Office. Only by the casting vote of the Labour chairman, Mr Arthur Bottomley, did the members excise the sentence, 'The Foreign Secretary's policies are totally negative. His pessimism and lack of ideas or initiatives is profoundly depressing.'

The committee's conclusion was that: 'Britain had a legal right to intervene, she had a moral obligation to intervene, she had the military capacity to intervene. She did not intervene for reasons which the Government refuses to give.'

To do nothing *is* a policy. As Lord Caradon, former Governor of Cyprus and the former British ambassador to the United Nations, put it, 'All the evil subsequently flowed from that decision, taken under United States influence, to let it run.'

James Callaghan was not as ignorant as he chose to appear. But an affectation of ignorance was a necessity for anyone who had taken Dr Kissinger's assurances at face value.

Ankara

After the 1960 London–Zurich agreements, which permitted both Greece and Turkey to station military forces on the island, the Turkish liaison officer in Cyprus was Colonel Turgut Sunalp. In this capacity he was involved in designing contingency plans for a Turkish military intervention and in helping the Turkish Cypriot leadership to develop an armed wing.

In November 1983 Turgut Sunalp was the leader of the inaptly named 'National Democracy Party', one of the three tightly controlled political formations which were allowed by the military junta to contest a carefully organized 'election'. His party enjoyed the open support and patronage of the real rulers of Turkey, the junta which had vetted the contending parties (disqualifying most of them), extended martial law, written a press code forbidding any criticism of military rule, and subjected dissidents to torture, exile and execution. A leading member of this five-man junta was General Necmettin Ersin, who had commanded the Turkish invasion forces in Cyprus in 1974.

Shortly before the 'election' took place, a letter was smuggled out of a detention camp near Istanbul and published in the Western press. It had been signed by almost all the leaders of the legitimate pre-junta political parties. (Bulent Ecevit, who did not sign it, had already been imprisoned separately for his criticism of military rule.) Among the signatories were Suleyman Demirel, leader of the conservative Justice Party and six times Prime Minister of Turkey since 1965, Denyz Baykal, a leader of the social democratic Republican People's Party and a former Finance Minister, and Ihsan Caglayangil, a former Justice Party Foreign Minister. Thirteen other former ministers of both parties added their names to the letter.

The elections, wrote these veterans, would be a sham. 'The Turkish people will vote only for the candidates selected by the junta . . . an insult to the country, to the nation and to the Turkish armed forces.' The country, they added, 'has been pushed into a heavier crisis than it was before 12 September 1980' – the date of the military coup. A telling phrase came towards the end of the letter, when Demirel, Baykal, Caglayangil and their *confrères* wrote: 'Turkey is not Pakistan. We are not looking for a Zia ul-Haq.'

A few days after the elections took place (and after the muzzled electorate had taken its revenge on Mr Sunalp's pro-junta party by relegating it to third place) the junta joined with Mr Rauf Denktash in proclaiming a Turkish separatist state in northern Cyprus. The nominal 'winner' of the election, Mr Turgut Ozal, was not informed of the move. The only foreign government to welcome it – even though it stopped short of outright recognition – was the dictatorial regime of General Zia ul-Haq in Pakistan.

This little bouquet of ironies is intended to give some idea of the relationship between the Cyprus imbroglio and the rise of authoritarianism in Turkey. When I first visited Turkish-occupied Cyprus, every public office and official building had a photograph of Bulent Ecevit – hero of the 1974 'peace operation' – on the wall. The day after his arrest and imprisonment – for criticizing the political arrogance of the very generals he had uncaged – every picture of Ecevit disappeared. The average, honest Turkish citizen may regard Cyprus as a straightforward case of defending an embattled Turkish minority. But it has always been rather more than that, and Turkey is now suffering the consequences of allowing Cyprus to help incubate an ambitious and chauvinistic military caste.

Since Turkey in a sense 'won' the 1974 military round, there was no national inquest of the kind that took place in a humiliated Greece, a devastated Cyprus, an embarrassed Britain or a compromised America. It is possible to describe only relatively piecemeal the way in which Cyprus brought the army and the Right back to power.

In 1970 the Turkish army mounted a coup in Ankara. It did so ostensibly in response to growing discontent in the Kurdish provinces of the country (which do not exist as officially Kurdish, since the Turkish Establishment has a rather callous attitude to non-Cypriot and non-Turkish minorities). The military regime also set itself to halt the Leftward drift among the urban poor, the trade unions and the large number of unemployed and discontented students (many of whom had resorted to ugly Baader-Meinhof types of extremism). The army has had an unusual place in Turkish politics since the time of Ataturk. It has not infrequently acted as a force in favour of democratic rule, replacing and disciplining oligarchs or incompetents who have misused their trust. One such occasion was its move against Adnan Menderes and Fatin Zorlu, hard-liners on Cyprus in the 1950s, who were overthrown and hanged in 1960 for their numerous depredations.

During the subsequent two decades, however, the army began to lose the image of the 'people's militia' and to become more technological, more stratified and more corrupt. It even set up a holding company named OYAK; a unit trust for officers, financed by a percentage of each officer's salary. OYAK took shares in Turkish and foreign enterprises, issuing a dividend to each officer and binding the army, in an almost feudal and guild sense, to Turkey's protection-minded and conservative possessing class. Milo Minderbinder could have done no better.

In these circumstances, then, the military regime of 1970–72 was not a success. It was very narrowly based, and resorted increasingly to torture and repression in order to get its way. Failing even in this, it decided rather grudgingly to relinquish power to the political parties. Bulent Ecevit, who had been the most outspoken critic of the ruling junta, won a large following for his courage in doing so and became almost the natural leader of subsequent coalition politics. The army seemed discredited as a power above society and faction.

It was Cyprus which restored the military to a point where it could pose, once again, as a champion of Turkey and the nation. The written record of 1974 shows that it was the armed forces which pushed, at every stage, for a policy of force and conquest. It was the Turkish Security Council (Guvenlik Kurulu) and not the cabinet or the parliament, which took the major decisions and which issued the crucial orders.

On 15 July, the date of the Ioannides–Sampson coup in Cyprus, Denyz Baykal and Bulent Ecevit talked with the General Staff at a Security Council meeting. Baykal (today under house arrest on the orders of these same generals) made a speech which canvassed the possibility of intervention. As Mehmet Ali Birand records the occasion: 'Ecevit posed the key question to the Generals – In how many days would you be ready? The answer was definite – We can begin the operation on Saturday morning.' The cabinet, meeting on the floor below, was informed of this decision at one o'clock in the morning. There were protests. 'You are taking decisions upstairs and then announcing them to us. Is this appropriate?'

In subsequent meetings of political and party leaders, even the conservative Demirel was dubious about a full-scale invasion, which he thought might brand Turkey internationally as a bully and an aggressor. He was supported, in this misgiving, by Nihat Erim, another ex-Prime Minister and head of the presidential group appointed to the Turkish Senate. Erim, a venerable jurist who had served in 1960 as a member of the Cyprus Joint Constitutional Committee, saw a trap: 'The United States might be behind this coup. Even if it is not certain yet, I sense that Washington has a positive attitude towards Sampson.'

Erim spoke, perhaps, more truly than he knew. Turkey was to become the executor for a policy it had not designed. Still, the combined weight of the chauvinist parties, especially Mr Necmettin Erbakan's National Salvation Party, and the armed forces, was enough to silence or confuse the doubters. Admiral Karacan (see p. 96) warned Ecevit that neither of them would survive a failure to act. Mr Muftuoglu of the National Salvation Party went one better when, as a member of the Turkish delegation at the Geneva talks, he threatened to kill himself if withdrawal from the first invasion beach-heads was agreed.

His zeal was supererogatory. The Turkish documents show that the first invasion led ineluctably to the second, and that the generals knew it. For a while, Ecevit and Baykal stressed 'the independence of Cyprus' as their goal, and talked of 'geographical federation'. They tried to hold back the Salvationists and the 'Grey Wolves' who insisted on immediate *taksim* (partition) or even on outright conquest of Cyprus. The die was probably cast by General Sancar, Chief of the General Staff, who in a message to the troops on 2 August, while negotiations on the first landing were still in progress, said: 'The duty of the army in Cyprus is not over yet.'

The rest is history. Ecevit became the victim of the forces he had set in motion. Despite his temporary and hysterical popularity, he was replaced within a few months by a coalition of the Rightist parties which had, in different ways, supported him over Cyprus. They had supported him, it turns out, as the rope supports a hanging man.

Restored to the centre of Turkish politics, and garlanded by their easy triumph in Cyprus, the generals began to take a more activist role. Long before they took formal control of the country in 1980, they had begun to administer martial law in several provinces – especially the Kurdish ones – and several cities. They had also placed limits on the ability of civilian politicians to negotiate even a partial Cyprus settlement. Time and again, members of the General Staff announced in ringing tones that the flag of Turkey, once planted, would not be withdrawn one inch. On more than one occasion, this rhetoric destroyed discussions about limited and palliative measures such as the return of Famagusta to its Greek Cypriot inhabitants.

Throughout the remainder of the 1970s, Turkey continued to be rent apart by religious and factional warfare, in which all kinds of dubious external influences could be guessed at. The figure of Mehmet Ali Agca, would-be assassin of Pope John Paul II, has become symbolic of this period. He was a Fascist, and a gunslinging member of Colonel Turkes's 'Grey Wolf' paramilitary youth. He was also available for 'contract' work in the *demi-monde* of extortion, narcotics and gun-running. He is the likely culprit in the murder of Adi Ipecki, editor of the distinguished liberal Establishment newspaper *Milliyet*. He also seems to have had connections with the colder world of Bulgarian intelligence services.

This impression, of a collusion between the extreme Right and the extreme Left against the democratic centre, led many people to welcome or at least to excuse the Turkish Military coup of 12 September 1980. Unlike the coup in Greece of 21 April 1967, this was not obviously the work of a clique of greedy and fanatical officers. Rather, it appeared to be the Turkish army exerting itself in defence of 'national unity'. There was, undoubtedly, a strong initial popular support for such a move. This took some time to wear off, as it became apparent that the army was planning to institute permanent authoritarian rule in a quasi-civilian guise.

It became clear early on that the junta was not impartial between the terrorists of Right and Left. The parties of the Left, and their affiliated trade unions and institutes, were simply abolished. Manifestations of Kurdish nationalism were mercilessly suppressed. The first daily newspaper to be closed entirely was *Aydinlik*, which had been temporarily shut down in 1974 because of its opposition to the invasion of Cyprus, and which had published a series of articles on the links between the extreme Right in Turkey, their counterparts among the Cypriot Turks, and certain groups within the Turkish army. The Turkish Peace Association, a group of veteran diplomats and political figures, attracted international sympathy during its show trial and the subsequent arbitrary imprisonment of its leaders. Among its 'crimes' had been attendance at a meeting in Athens where it voted for a resolution concerning the 'integrity' of Cyprus. This counted as 'slandering the Turkish nation'.

The Right were dealt with more leniently. Their terror activities ceased. These had, after all, achieved their objective of bringing about a military government, and their cessation allowed the junta to claim credit for the reduction in violence. Turkes's party ideologue, Dr Oktay Agah Guner, is out on bail despite the fact that he faces capital charges. He has appeared at a number of public seminars designed to justify junta policies. An example had to be made of Colonel Turkes himself, because his involvement in violence had been so notorious. While awaiting his trial (still inconclusive at the time of writing, and in any case more than many of his opponents have had) the colonel wrote to General Kenan Evren, head of the junta, asking plaintively, 'Why am I in detention while my ideas are in power?' Turkes might have studied the history of the German SA with some profit, as Ecevit might have studied the history of German Social Democracy. Thugs are dispensable once they have facilitated the seizure of power, and so are 'reformers' who vote for war credits.

Shortly after the Turkish junta took power, a document from the Turkish General Staff was given to me by a senior military source. It is headed, 'Turkish Republic. Official'. It is issued by 'The Directorate of War History of the General Staff'. It is printed by the General Staff and is entitled, 'Greek–Turkish Relations and the Megali Idea'. It was written before the coup, and gives an unusually revealing insight into the ideas that animated those who carried it out. Its concluding section, which sets out Turkish ambitions in the Aegean, would certainly lend weight to Colonel Turkes's question. Designed for the instruction of Turkish officers, and classified as highly confidential, its conclusion (here published for the first time) is:

> If a state outside NATO was to attack the Dodecanese, including Samothrace, Mytilene, Chios and Samos, it would be difficult or impossible for Greece to defend these islands. The following facts show that any Greek resistance would be impossible: these islands are situated very far from Greece and the despatch of forces from the mother country for their defence would be very difficult – even more so because one of the conditions of the Treaty of Lausanne is that they remain unfortified.
>
> An intervention by a country outside NATO or the occupation of these islands, which are very near Turkey, by

another country, may not result in a crisis in so far as Greece is concerned. But from the point of view of a Turkish defence of Anatolia this would create a strategic and tactical diversion and would also cause our economic isolation.

The Aegean, since it affects the interests and the security of many countries, may become an area of friction. Greece does not have the power or the potential to secure peace in the Aegean. This situation does not accord with the plans and the defensive objectives of NATO, which aims to preserve international peace. It endangers its defence.

For this reason, NATO should pay attention to the rights and memoranda of Turkey, which is more reliable and not unstable like Greece (which changes its position to promote its own interests). *From the point of view of Turkish security, apart from the existing borders, there is need to establish an area of security which would include the nearby islands.* [italics mine]

There is an older example. When the Dodecanese were under Italian occupation, during Mussolini's aggressive policy towards Turkey, military camps and hospitals were set up in Rhodes and Leros. The most important parts of the islands were fortified and Turkey was being threatened, from very nearby, over many years.

Turkey today, with a population of 40 million and a large and strong army, faced with the creation of a military iron ring extending from the Aegean to the south and including Cyprus, and faced with the cutting off of the Aegean and the Mediterranean nautical routes, cannot tolerate such a situation. Nor could any other state in a similar position.

The examination of this obviously harmful Greek position; harmful because of its recent behaviour; and the strong affirmation of Turkish rights in the Aegean, on a solid basis, would solve the strategic problems of the region.

The Turkish authorities here make it clear that they regard Cyprus and the Aegean as possible if not actual Turkish possessions. They suit their actions to their words by building and maintaining an 'Army of the Aegean', heavily equipped and well accoutred with landing craft, in their southern ports.

This army and fleet is outside the formal command of NATO.

Since 1974, when American military aid to Turkey was $196 million, it has climbed to over $760 million and next year will touch the billion mark. This aid, which helps to confirm the army in power and which spurs Greece into an economically beggaring regional arms race, is helping to aggrandize the Turkish military, helping to consolidate its presence in Cyprus, outweighing the stated wishes of Congress about a Cyprus settlement, and enhancing the risk of an Aegean war. It is also postponing the day when Turks will once again be freely allowed to vote. As was once said of Prussia, Turkey is not a country that has an army, but an army that has a country. The 1974 invasion of Cyprus uncorked the genie, and helped to raise the curtain on this dismal scene. Most Turks remain confident that their government did the right thing in Cyprus. It has taken time to make it clear that a nation oppressing others cannot itself be free.

Coda: the Kissinger Version

Throughout the second half of this account, the figure of Henry Kissinger has been decisive. It was Kissinger who decided to let the coup against Makarios go ahead, Kissinger who tried to screen the Greek junta from the fatal consequences of that policy, Kissinger who engineered and led the switch to Turkey when both of these expedients failed, and Kissinger who persuaded the British government to renege on its treaty obligations. This may seem to pile too much responsibility on one man. But, in an oblique way, Dr Kissinger himself confirms the analysis. Normally, in his published writings and memoirs, he places himself at the centre of the stage. This is especially so, as Seymour Hersh notes, when there is anything like a success to be claimed. But in his narrative of the Cyprus crisis, Kissinger almost effaces himself. This may well be because, as President Kennedy put it ruefully after the Bay of Pigs, 'Success has many fathers. Failure is an orphan.'

We are privileged in having Dr Kissinger's own affidavit about Cyprus. It appears in his book *Years of Upheaval*, a work dealing with the years 1972 to 1976. Kissinger begins his passage on the 1974 crisis with one apology and one evasion. The apology comes when he mentions, 'the vulnerabilities of a divided administration with a President in no position to impose coherence', as if Cyprus was something that happened to him rather than he to Cyprus. He does not mention the pre-existing support of that administration for the Greek junta, and he treats Watergate, too, as if it was something that befell Nixon rather than something which he originated. Then comes the evasion: 'I must leave a full discussion of the Cyprus episode to another occasion, for it stretched into the Ford presidency and its legacy exists unresolved today.' This is unusually coy. Dr Kissinger discusses Vietnam, Cambodia, the Middle East, Angola, Chile and the SALT treaty with great brio and inventiveness in the very same book. Of all these topics it might be said that their 'legacies' existed 'unresolved today', and of all of them it is superfluous to the point of fatuity to say that they 'stretched' into the exiguous Ford presidency.

There follows a congested and ignorant summary of Graeco–Turkish relations since the Byzantine epoch. It fails to mention the Greek war of independence but it does say, in a moment of racialist condescension that, after 1920: 'The two nations continued to coexist (if that is the word), the Greeks remembering Turkey's military predominance, the Turks obsessed by their fear of Greek intellectual subtlety . . . the Greek–Turkish conflict has belonged to the blood feuds of history.'

This trite and tiring style has its counterpart in Kissinger's superficial analysis. He blames the entirety of intercommunal strife in Cyprus on Makarios (who is never in this chapter dignified with the title of President) and ends that insultingly brief passage by saying that: 'I had always taken it for granted that the next intercommunal crisis in Cyprus would provoke Turkish intervention.'

To the extent that this breezy, omniscient statement is true (which it is not, because the 1974 events were not 'intercommunal') it is fair to ask what Kissinger thought he was doing when he encouraged a Greek junta policy that was designed to bring about such a crisis. He is not good enough to tell us – the chapter is full of ellipses – but even his omissions are illuminating, as are his flagrant misrepresentations of July 1974:

> Greece was a military dictatorship; hence, all groups critical
> of our approach to human rights urged us to turn on it as the
> instigator of the upheaval; failure in Cyprus would, it was
> hoped, produce the overthrow of the hated Greek Colonels.
> This view was held passionately not only among traditional
> opponents of Nixon; it was the dominant conviction in the
> State Department; the Secretary of Defense moved toward it
> increasingly as the week progressed.
>   To me, the issue was more complicated. I thought it most
> unlikely that Turkey would tolerate the union of Cyprus with
> Greece. That Turkey was driving toward a showdown was
> obvious – at least to me.

Here we find an almost classic distillation of the Kissinger
method. First, there is a daring and tremendous *non-sequitur*. It
was the Greek junta which wanted, or said it wanted, 'the union
of Cyprus with Greece'. Its opponents, in the United States and
everywhere else, wanted Cyprus to be *independent.* Kissinger
cannot possibly have been unaware of this. Second, there is the
suggestion that Kissinger's was the only cool head among these
'passionate' folk; the only one to appreciate how 'complicated'
everything was. Third, there is the usual attempt to shift
responsibility elsewhere in the bureaucracy (if the Defense and
State Departments really did want to be rid of the Greek
Colonels, by the way, they had a strange way of showing it).
Finally comes the hindsight dressed up as prediction; the
Turkish drive 'toward a showdown'. If Kissinger was so sure
about this impending 'drive', and he may have been, then it
remains to be explained why he worked so hard to allay the fear
of it at the time. All that he accomplishes by this passage is the
counterfeiting of the intended as the inevitable.
    Kissinger unintentionally validates this criticism one para-
graph later, when he writes, absurdly in view of the foregoing,
that: 'Turkey's demands left little doubt that it was planning to
intervene. Explicit condemnation of the Greek junta by the
United States would have turned a likelihood into a certainty.'
This is an abject denial of responsibility, as well as an

astounding denial of the facts. It was the *refusal* of the British and American governments to isolate the junta that freed Turkey, both militarily and some might say morally, to intervene alone. It was not until he had failed to secure such joint condemnation and co-ordination that the crafty Bulent Ecevit gave his generals the signal to invade.

Kissinger, having put both hands on the tar-baby, now uses both feet to try to prise them off. He goes on to recount:

> My view, as I was to explain to a WSAG meeting of July 21 [Washington Special Action Group; a Nixon-inspired committee set up in 1969 to by-pass the cabinet in foreign-policy making] was that the Greek government was unlikely to survive its follies. That made it all the more necessary that the United States not be seen in Greece as the agent of its humiliation. At the same time, we could not without cost resist a Turkish invasion because that would be considered as objectively supporting the Greek junta.

No great foresight was required to predict an event (the fall of the junta) which in fact took place the following day. Again, one notices the circular Kissinger version appearing as a sort of pedagogic obverse of the truth. The United States was already considered, by 21 July, to be 'the agent of Greece's humiliation'. It had been considered as such, by many Greek democrats, for the preceding seven years. What Kissinger does not know, or else cannot admit, is that it was precisely the Cyprus disaster – the coup against Makarios – which most Greeks felt as the humiliation. Having either wilfully or accidentally misunderstood this, but having in any case ignored it, Dr Kissinger's second falsification is only symmetrical with the first. It was the Greek democrats, not the Greek junta, who implored help to oppose the Turkish landing. By a sleight of hand which uses 'Greece' to mean 'all Greeks' or, according to taste, 'the Greek junta', Dr Kissinger abolishes an important distinction which, in real life, he understood only too well.

The same absence of discrimination can be observed in the way Kissinger dodges the issue of the Turkish invasion. By the time of the WSAG meeting which he cites, the first wave of

Turks was already ashore. There was almost a full month to go before that army launched its second invasion and occupied the north. The Greek junta fell the day after the WSAG meeting. Even if one admits the doubtful hypothesis that American opposition to the first invasion (academic by 21 July) could be construed as 'objectively supporting the Greek junta', how is it possible to argue this in the case of the *second* invasion? The final touch is added to this reasoning by the fact that Dr Kissinger was already seen, quite correctly, as an 'objective' (as well as subjective) supporter of the junta.

On the next page, Kissinger remarks with clumsy sarcasm that: 'On July 22, the junta in Athens was overthrown and replaced by a democratic government under the distinguished conservative leader Constantine Karamanlis. Within days the mood in America changed. The very groups that had castigated us for our reluctance to assault Greece now wanted us to go into all-out opposition to Turkey.'

This is a revealing paragraph, with another self-evident *non-sequitur*. Had Kissinger mentioned the fact that there were pro-junta and anti-Turkish organizations in the United States, he would have been on safer ground. He does not do so, arguably because such groups had been loyal Nixon allies in the Greek–American community. He implies instead that there was some inconsistency in those Democrats who first opposed the junta and then opposed the Turkish army. Any irony involved here is at Dr Kissinger's expense, since he himself changed from supporting the Greek junta to supporting the Turkish army and changed, on his own account, during the one night between the WSAG meeting and the final collapse of the Ioannides dictatorship.

A close scrutiny of Kissinger's memoirs confirms what a careful study of the actual events has already shown. There was, indeed, a 'double tilt' in United States policy that summer. It was a 'tilt' against democracy, against international law and against the principle of non-aggression. It is to the credit of those who opposed it that their chief antagonist has to resort to such lies and half-truths in order to counter their objections. There were many suspicions about Dr Kissinger's role at the time, and there have been many since. There is unusual importance, therefore, in his giving a testimonial to his own duplicity.

Alternatives: Crete and the Hatay

In one respect, Dr Kissinger and others do have a point. There is a nationalistic element in the Cyprus equation. It is not as strong or as essential as it is represented to be, by those who wish to blame only the victims for their misfortunes. But it is present. Both Turks and Greeks have vivid national memories, and in both cases one national memory contains dire reflections about the other. Even though there were no serious conflicts between Greek and Turkish Cypriots until the present generation, the competing ideas of Hellenism and Turkism are rooted in the events of the past.

Very roughly speaking, the Turks fear another Crete and the Greeks fear another Alexandretta. To understand this, it is necessary to remember that most Greek and Turkish triumphs have been at the expense of the other. Even Greece's finest hour – her wartime resistance in the years when Turkey was neutral – led ultimately to a post-war acquisition of islands which Turkey regarded as her own, or at least as non-Greek.

Crete: The long struggle to unite Crete with Greece was considered morally and politically justifiable by the major European powers of the day, which is why in the end it was successful. During the lengthy period of Turkish occupation, many Cretans, like their Cypriot counterparts, had undergone either coercive or submission conversion to Islam. And many Turks had been settled in Crete by the Ottoman authorities. The battle for *enosis* waged by the Greek majority was very protracted and bitter. The Cretans joined the Greek revolution of 1821, but were brutally put down by Ibrahim Pasha and briefly ceded to Egyptian rule by way of Turkish compensation to Mohammed Ali for his help. Having reverted to Turkish control, the island remained in a state of unrest which culminated in the famous rising of 1866. (It was during this revolt that Abbot Mareses of Arkadion blew up his monastery

rather than surrender it, and thus gave the island its motto of
'Freedom or Death'.) The revolt was one of those, like Ireland
in 1916 or Paris in 1871, which fail militarily but succeed in
kindling a political idea. Turkey began to talk of 'modifications'
to its rule, and to waver in the application of force. A later
rebellion, in May 1896, led to a brief war between Greece and
Turkey and to the end of formal Turkish rule over the island.
The European powers intervened with two objectives: to
conclude the unstable and unjustifiable Turkish satrapy, and to
forestall the union of Crete with Greece. Like Cyprus, Crete
became nominally independent, with a predominantly Greek
population and a Turkish Muslim minority of about one-ninth.
Like Cyprus, its status was officially guaranteed by foreign
troops. As in the case of Cyprus, both communities regarded
the settlement, in different ways, as provisional. The Turkish
Muslims rebelled in 1898, firing on the British contingent at
Candia and launching a pogrom against the local Christians.
This achieved the opposite effect of the one intended (which
was a renewed Turkish intervention), in that it goaded the
European powers to demand the final withdrawal of all Turkish
troops. This duly took place, and was shortly afterwards
followed by an exodus of Muslim Turks to Asia Minor. It would
be euphemistic in the extreme to describe this exodus as
voluntary. Many Cretans took the opportunity to revenge
themselves on their former superiors and conquerors. It was
only a matter of time before full *enosis* with Greece was
accomplished, and Crete became Greek in 1913. To this day it
remains a stronghold of radical, republican politics and a
consistent source of support for Greek leaders who take a tough
line with Turkey.

The Turkish Cypriot leadership often cites Crete as precisely
the precedent it seeks to avoid. It uses Cretan history to give
depth and force to its claim that the Greeks want not just the
union of Cyprus with 'Hellenism' but the removal or destruction of the Turkish minority. It also, privately, invokes the
Cretan example in its opposition to the 'internationalization' of
the Cyprus question. Efforts by the United Nations or any other
concert of powers are viewed with suspicion, because they may
provide 'cover' for a Greek *fait accompli*. British colonial rule

was supported by the Turks because they considered it an insurance against precisely this outcome. The Turkish army's presence, and the virtual absorption of northern Cyprus by Turkey, is considered an even more durable guarantee. In giving what I think is a fair *précis* of this attitude, I aim to do no more than explain it.

The Hatay: Greeks have many racial and national memories of Turkish rule and Turkish force, but the example that is most pertinent to Cyprus does not directly involve the modern Greek world. Just across the water from Cyprus, in the top right corner of the Mediterranean, lies the port of Alexandretta, known in Turkish as Iskenderun. It is the capital of the province of the Hatay. It was in this port among others that the Turkish invasion force was prepared in 1960, and finally despatched to Cyprus in 1974.

Until 1939 Alexandretta and the Hatay were part of Syria. But there was a significant Turkish minority both in the city and in the province, with sixty per cent of the population being either Arabs or Armenians. Under the Franco–Turkish accords of 1921, the Hatay was part of the French mandate in Syria. In one of his very rare flirtations with irredentism, Kemal Ataturk demanded that the province be ceded to Turkey. The Syrians were utterly opposed to such a demand, first because the Turks were a minority and second because Alexandretta was the chief lifeline port for northern Syria and the important city of Aleppo. The Syrians, however, did not enjoy self-government.

France was inclined to conciliate Ataturk. It wanted to conclude a military alliance with Turkey against Germany. In 1937, one year after the French announced plans for a qualified independence for Syria, they also proclaimed 'autonomy' for the Hatay. The province was to have internal self-government. Turkish would be an official language along with Arabic. Syria would be responsible for its foreign affairs and would be linked with it by a customs and monetary union. Like Cyprus in 1960, the Hatay was to award both sides their second-best aspirations. Like Cyprus, the Hatay did not remain at rest for very long. When the League of Nations sent an election commission to the province, and found that the Turkish voters were in a minority,

Ataturk moved troops up to the border in protest. He also
organized angry rioting by the minority. The French, still
anxious to appease Turkey and having no fellow-feeling for
Arab nationalist sentiment, agreed to let Turkish soldiers share
in the policing of the Hatay, and made them joint guarantors of
its autonomy in July 1938. That was enough. New electoral
registers were drawn up in haste and in the following month of
August, with Turkish soldiers looking on, an election produced
a wafer-thin Turkish majority. Exercising their right of self-
determination, the Turks then announced that the Hatay was a
fully independent republic. Within a year, on 29 June 1939,
they proclaimed its union with Turkey. (Ataturk, who had died
on 10 November 1938, might or might not have thought this
haste a little blatant.) The Armenians of the Hatay needed little
encouragement to leave. Many Arabs did likewise. Syria has
never forgiven this sleight of hand by the Turks and the French.
Turkey did sign an *entente* with France in October 1939,
but then prudently stayed neutral throughout the Second
World War.

Many Greek Cypriots see this episode as the classic use by
Turkey of a 'strategic minority' to advance its own claims and
expand its own territory, much as the Germans used the
Sudeten minority in Czechoslovakia. They note the progression
of demands from 'autonomy' to 'partnership' to 'independence'
and finally to annexation. They also note the way in which the
international community acquiesced in the process out of a
desire to appease Turkey. In the present circumstances, with
the Turkish mainland population expanding at an extraordinary
rate, and with its strategic position in the Cold War giving
Turkey a strong leverage on the West, the Greek Cypriots
wonder if they, too, are not marked down for the Alexandretta
treatment. It has already happened in the north. Is it intended
to stop there?

Of these two 'worst-case' alternatives (to borrow a handy but
inelegant phrase from American political science) it is clear that
the Hatay example is the one nearest to contemporary reality.
The Turks may justify what they have done by reference to any

number of real or exaggerated past fears. Yet the proclamation of a separate Turkish Cypriot state in November 1983 was clearly a move towards full absorption by Turkey. That would be enough in itself to create alarm. But the political groups which, in Turkey and in Turkish Cyprus, had agitated for a declaration of 'independence' by Mr Denktash were the same forces which have been pressing for the Turkish army to 'finish the job' and take the whole island.

The London *Financial Times* reported from Ankara, on 6 December 1983, that,

> in choosing to allow the declaration of independence by Mr Rauf Denktash, the Turkish Cypriot leader, to go ahead, Turkey's leaders are pointing to a radically new view, not only of the Cyprus dispute but of Turkey's overall quarrel with Greece . . . Turkey now sees southern Cyprus and the Aegean Dodecanese islands as post-Ottoman areas inhabited by Greeks but with unresolved status to some degree, because they continue to generate military and political problems for the Turkish republic.

The writer of this report (which electrified Athens when it was published) made it clear that the Treaty of Lausanne, which established the existing balance of forces between Greece and Turkey in the eastern Aegean, was considered by the Turkish leadership to be a 'disappointment'. This means that, semi-officially at least, Turkey is not satisfied with its gains in Cyprus.

What of the Cretan model? Whereas the Turkish Cypriot authorities maintain that 'Greeks and Turks cannot live together' and excludes even people of Greek descent, or Greek Cypriots with British or other passports from its territory, the Republic of Cyprus has made no move to abolish Turkish Cypriot rights. Whatever may have been the mistakes and crimes of the past, the government holds the abandoned property of Turkish Cypriots in trust for them. All Cypriots, according to law, have the right to return to their homes. Even the fact that Greek refugees have been settled provisionally on Turkish property does not alter this legal position.

The Turks maintain that the Greeks have never abandoned the *Megali Idea*; the dream of a reborn Byzantine Empire with its capital in Constantinople. It is logically impossible to refute a suspicion. The fact that there is no political party or movement in Greece which advocates such a policy, and the fact that even Brigadier Ioannides was unable to convince his fellow-dictators to act upon it, does not convince the Turkish critic.

Many Greeks believe that Turkey not only covets the Aegean islands closest to its coast, but actually plans to take them by force. The evidence here is suggestive rather than conclusive. Before the abolition of independent political parties in Turkey, there was at least one, the National Action Party, which called for a Greater Turkey extended in all directions, including Cyprus and the Aegean. There have been, as above, many unguarded statements from generals and politicians to the same effect. Documents and books used in the training of Turkish officers make out the Greek claim to the islands to be spurious (see pages 145–6). It may be that in some remote garrison there is a young Turkish lieutenant who broods on one day becoming the saviour of his country – a Turkish Ioannides.

All this tends outside the scope of this book. But Cyprus remains as the symbol of unresolved Greek and Turkish conflict. It symbolizes, for the Greeks, what Andreas Papandreou has called the 'shrinkage of Hellenism' – the pushing of Greeks and Greek life out of Asia Minor and Constantinople that took place in living memory. The Greek Cypriots who were evicted from the north of Cyprus, and their fellows who are now forbidden even to visit it, will continue to call their old villages and towns by their original names. They will have a memory more recent than Smyrna in 1922 and more vivid and bitter even than Istanbul in 1955. They will not acknowledge the legitimacy of the occupation, and nor will their children. If there was a time when the Greeks were insensitive to the susceptibilities of the Turks, now the Turks behave as if Greek feelings do not count. Those who have encouraged this development from outside can now glibly refer to it as 'a lethal cocktail' (Henry Kissinger, *Years of Upheaval*).

VI Conclusion

On the third day – and final morning – the Archbishop and I had a quiet talk alone in his study. Rather whimsically, he said, 'I like you, Mr Secretary, you speak candidly and I respect that. It's too bad we couldn't have met under happier circumstances. Then, I'm sure, we could have been friends.' A brief pause and then he said, 'We've talked about many things and we've been frank with one another. I think it right to say that we've developed a considerable rapport. Yet there's one thing I haven't asked you and I don't know whether I should or not, but I shall anyway. Do you think I should be killed by the Turks or the Greeks? Better by the Greeks, wouldn't you think?'

'Well,' I replied, 'I agree that we've talked frankly to one another about many things and that we have established a rapport. But as to the matter you've just raised with me, Your Beatitude, that's your problem!'

George Ball, *The Past Has Another Pattern*

Afterwards, Ball made no secret of his unforgiving resentment of Makarios's role in 1964. During a Brookings Institution conference in 1969, Ball said in the presence of State Department colleagues, 'That son of a bitch Makarios will have to be killed before anything happens in Cyprus.'

Laurence Stern, *The Wrong Horse*

The owl of Minerva, said Hegel, takes wing only at dusk. Students of his difficult and idealistic theory of history take this to mean that only when an epoch is closed can it be properly understood. Hegel, of course, thought that the only thing to be learned from history was that nobody did learn from history. The Cyprus problem is rich in support for his view. But a certain dusk, not yet night, has fallen across the island, and it might not be impertinent to try and deduce some lessons.

The Cyprus problem consists of not one, but four, related questions. The most important of these is the relationship between Greek and Turkish Cypriots, which sets the difficult conundrum: can two widely separated national groups find a peaceful coexistence involving two languages, two religions and two interpretations of history?

The second, which is related but by no means identical, makes Cyprus the site of a longstanding difference between two great states: Greece and Turkey, both inheritors of vast, bygone empires. It is unlikely that the future of the island can be divorced from the wider settlement of differences between these larger rivals.

The third element is one of time rather than place. Cyprus came to independence during the Cold War, which has made every country in the world a place of conflict between the superpowers. Ideological commitments are strong in the island, but have not proved strong enough to transcend the first two tensions.

Finally, there is an element involving place rather than time. Cyprus occupies a strategic position in the Levant, and outside powers have never scrupled to employ local and regional rivalries in order to get their own way there. It is this, last, factor combined with the second one which has promoted Cyprus, like Lebanon, from a local dispute to an actual and potential international confrontation. It is this aspect, also, which has made it possible to give the wishes of its inhabitants such a lowly place on the order of priorities, and often impossible to 'synchronize' better inter-communal relations with better Greek–Turkish mainland relations.

Now that the debris of the 1974 explosion has settled, and now that some of those responsible have either stood trial or published their memoirs, it has become possible to attempt some conclusions. Mine are that Cyprus was plunged into war by the operations of the fourth element on the first and second – with the third element acting as an occasional incitement or justification. The Greek Cypriots would be mistaken in blaming all the disasters that have overtaken them on outside meddling. But they have considerable warrant for doing so. Turkish Cypriot propagandists, who hasten to blame everything on Greek ambition, ignore the fact that they, too, have been used and exploited by powers larger than themselves.

Many outsiders have accused the Greek Cypriots of *hubris*; the sin of pride which tempts fate to take retribution. By behaving as if Turkey was four hundred miles away instead of forty they asked for trouble and (the outsider usually adds with satisfaction) they got it. In our day, as in classical antiquity, *hubris* is defined by the consequent *nemesis*. The trouble with this argument or method is that those who encounter *nemesis* are presumed to have done something to deserve it. Cyprus is the victim of a miserable fate, *ergo* there must have been a crime or an error which beckoned it on. This opinion, like the belief in original sin, is hard to rebut.

At almost every stage in the drama, however, the weaknesses or errors of Cypriots were exploited and compounded by external intervention. This was true when the British fomented intercommunal distrust, first to consolidate their rule and then to maintain it. It was true when the Turkish government organized an anti-Greek pogrom in Istanbul to bring pressure to bear on the Cyprus negotiations with London, and was rewarded with concessions. It was true when the Greek and Turkish governments put local extremists into commanding positions by giving them money and weapons. It was true when the Greek junta, itself the product of foreign intervention, decided to eliminate President Makarios. Perhaps most of all it was true when the United States government, in the words of George Ball, 'established an underground contact' with the terrorists of General Grivas, and did so in the name of protecting the Turks! In that incident, both ends were played against the middle and the manipulation of internal tensions was dovetailed with a great-power calculation designed to abolish the island's independence. From that incident, also, stems the foreign involvement with Greek-sponsored subversion in Cyprus, which led to the coup and to the Turkish invasion. When Makarios put his question to George Ball,

asking mischievously whether it would be Greeks or Turks who
would be set on to kill him, he was being shrewd and not, as the
unironic and literal Ball supposes, offensive. Mr Ball obviously
thinks that he comes well out of the exchange, or he would not
have published it. But his rejoinder is thunderously inept. It
was not Makarios's 'problem' whether he lived or died. It was
the responsibility of those who wished him ill, and Ball is at
least honest enough to make it plain that he was one of those.
His successors, especially in the Nixon administration, behaved
in such a way as to justify the Cypriot belief that foreign
meddling has been the chief problem at both the local and the
international levels. At the risk of overstressing the point, let
me just point out again that by helping General Grivas, Mr Ball
and his colleagues more or less ensured the animosity of the
Turkish Cypriots, who felt menaced by Grivas far more than
they felt threatened by Makarios. By helping further to poison
an ethnic conflict, the United States deliberately created the
very conditions which it was later to cite, hypocritically, as the
justification for partition. Where the British had made an
opportunistic use of Greek–Turkish rivalry and distrust, the
United States and its proxies made an instrument out of it.

> *Or l'essence d'une nation est que tous les individus aient*
> *beaucoup de choses en commun, et aussi que tous aient oublié*
> *bien des choses.*
>
> Ernest Renan, *Qu'est-ce qu'une nation*
> (With acknowledgements to Benedict Anderson)

Obviously, things *could* have been different. The navies of
the Catholic powers, later bombastically celebrated by G.K.
Chesterton, inflicted a shattering defeat on the Turks at
Lepanto in October 1571. If the victory had come three months
earlier, it might have raised the siege of Famagusta and
redeemed its commander Marcantonio Brigadino from the
necessity of being flayed alive, for the glory of Venice, by the
Turkish invader Lala Mustafa. Cyprus would never have
become Turkish. Alternatively, if the late Sultan had not been
so gullible, the island might never have passed from Turkey to
Britain. Again, if Britain had been more sincere, or Greece

more determined, then Cyprus might have achieved *enosis* long enough since for it to be uncontroversial today. Like Rhodes, it might even have got it without a fight. These are not the real 'ifs' in the present situation, though speculation about the latter ones can fill Greek Cypriots with alternating moods of sobriety and anger.

The real 'if' is the one which inquires of the Greek Cypriots, since they are the majority, whether they could have averted the frightful events of 1974. I have argued, I hope persuasively, that there were forces at work which would have victimized the Greek Cypriots whatever they did. This does not and should not free them from the obligation to consider their missed opportunities. These seem to cluster under four headings:

1. *Economics*. The Turkish Cypriots, despite their history of *political* and *national* privilege as an organized group, were most often *economically* underprivileged in the mass. During the period 1960–74, when the Greeks were morally and legally responsible, as the majority, for all citizens on the island, they gave this problem a low priority. Greek trade unionists made admirable efforts to enlist Turkish Cypriots as fellow-workers. But at central-government level there was a perceptible stinginess in allocating economic aid or in sharing resources for education, development and housing. This reproduced, in social terms, a version of the wider and deeper national problem. The Turks, who were a minority but whose leaders talked as a majority, were economic inferiors. While the Greeks, who were a majority in Cyprus but a minority in the region, were economic and entrepreneurial superiors. This jealousy only reinforced the 'double minority' problem of Cyprus, where each side felt itself the aggrieved party.

2. *Culture*. The Turks are a minority in Cyprus, but they are a Turkish minority. This makes them the heirs of a very strong and distinct national identity. Throughout the years of independence, the Makarios government failed to set up any institution specifically designed to meet Turkish needs. As Kyriakos Markides puts it in his book *The Rise and Fall of the Cyprus Republic*, 'Not a single committee of experts was established for the rational and systematic study and analysis of data relating to internal Turkish Cypriot and Turkish politics.'

And as Costa P. Kyrris of the Cyprus Research Centre put it in his estimable book *Peaceful Coexistence in Cyprus* (1977):

> The very fact that the present book, whatever its value, has been written only in 1976–77 instead of some sixty or eighty or at least thirty years ago, points to our belated realization of the crucial importance of systematic knowledge of our Turkish neighbours, their problems, mentality, origins and relations with us. This delay has been fatal for the inter-ethnic developments in the island.

Since 1974 there has been an upsurge of interest and feeling on this point among Greek Cypriots, but it is difficult not to agree with Mr Kyrris that it came rather late. Minerva's owl took wing only when the dusk was thickening.

Greek Cypriots are fond of quoting those British figures from the past, notably Sir Ronald Storrs, who were sensible enough to realize that if they *felt* themselves to be Greek, they *were* Greek. The same must be held to apply to the Turks. It is true that Cyprus has a long history of symbiosis, typical of Ottoman Asia Minor. There was for some time a local sect known as the *Linobambakoi* or in English 'linen-cottons' who, as their nickname implies, were dualists. They practised both Christian and Muslim rites, and each took both a Christian and a Muslim name. Perhaps as a partial result of this and other symbiotic elements, Turkish Cypriots had adopted the practice of giving themselves surnames long before Kemal Ataturk's reforms made the adoption of a surname obligatory on the mainland. Many Christian Cypriots converted to Islam under Ottoman rule, if only to escape the special taxes from which 'believers' were exempt. Several Turkish Cypriot villages bore the names of Christian saints as a result – or did until the enforced Turkification of place names by the Denktash regime.

All of this deserves to be remembered, as do the dozens of mixed villages that existed before the 1974 *apartheid* system was imposed. But the Turks, if only in response to the nationalist revolt among the Greeks, have taken to a more assertive definition of their Turkishness, and it is idle to pretend otherwise. You cannot make a child grow smaller, and the

Turkish Cypriots will not, whatever their disillusionment with Anatolian rule, voluntarily revert to the position they occupied before 1974. A future solution will depend largely on the intelligence of the Greeks (who also have little nostalgia for that period of junta menace) in recognizing this. It goes without saying that a Turkish occupation which prevents Greek and Turkish Cypriots from even meeting one another is the chief obstacle even to a consideration of this point.

3. *Religion*. There is every reason why the Orthodox Church should occupy a special place in Greek Cypriot life, since it has been one of the guardians and repositories of national feeling for centuries past. Yet the presence of a Greek ethnarch as simultaneous head of state made it that much more difficult for Turkish Cypriots to identify with the new order inaugurated by independence. With the accession of President Kyprianou, Church and state have become more separated. In retrospect, it would have been politic for Archbishop Makarios to have made more efforts in the same direction. A future unified Cyprus would have no choice but to be secular in politics and law.

4. *Military forces*. It was clearly a mistake ever to permit the stationing of foreign military forces on Cyprus. Archbishop Makarios once told me, when I asked him what he considered to have been his greatest error, that he most regretted allowing the Greek contingent to settle permanently on the island. We have seen how the Turks used a small, initial military presence to expand their army from a few enclaves across one-third of Cyprus. And the British bases have been used to assist in partitioning rather than securing the island. The bases have also acted as a constant temptation to outsiders to treat Cyprus as a tactical or strategic pawn rather than as a country with a complex individuality. They serve no purpose that cannot be discharged in another way, and the original reason for their presence – the safeguarding of British control over Suez, Jordan and Iraq – has long since evaporated. A unified Cyprus would require international guarantees of demilitarization, which would have to be complete if it was to have any point.

Having started with Milan Kundera's warning about amnesia, it may seem perverse to end with Renan's advice about forgetting. But, if Cyprus is to recover from the blows it has been dealt, it will have to acquire a common memory and this will mean less stress on individual or sectarian grievances. If people remember *everything*, they go mad. What needs to be remembered, set down and memorized, is the injury done to all Cypriots, to the common home, by distant, uncaring enemies.

One can write the word 'solution' glibly, at a time when such a term seems more Utopian than ever. The enemies of an independent Cyprus still seem overwhelmingly strong. Even if the neglected steps towards intercommunal composure had been taken in the brief and arduous years of independence, it is impossible to doubt that these enemies would have been just as assiduous. And one chauvinist or Fascist can destroy in one day (a rumour of rape, a fire in the church or mosque) what the inhabitants of a peaceful, integrated village have spent generations building.

Those who believe that the Cypriots 'brought it on themselves' have a duty to explain away the known facts of British colonial policy; the intrusion of the Greek junta and its backers; the creation by Ankara of an armed movement in favour of partition; and the declared desire of the United States government to 'remove' Makarios. These pressures, exerted on a small people with almost no defences of their own, were the major determining causes of the present misery.

This is not to say that the present misery is, in all its aspects, the intended result of outside interference. The Acheson–Ball partition might, if implemented to the strict letter, have been less outrageously inconsistent with demography than the *status quo*. But the policy and its implementation, both formulated without the consent of the Cypriots, cannot be so easily distinguished. The groups and parties who were chosen to bring about partition were violent, unstable and selfish. The responsibility for what occurred, then, rests with those who equipped and encouraged them. The apple did not fall very far from the tree.

I am confident that I will be accused of putting forward a 'conspiracy theory'. Actually, what I have argued is that there was collusion between unevenly matched and differently motivated forces, who for varying reasons feared or disliked an independent Cyprus. Ten years after the disaster, we know more than the victims did at the time. Nothing that has been published or uncovered since, however, contradicts the terrible suspicions that the victims had then. Those who deny the collusion theory; those who interpret events as a mere chapter of accidents, have a great deal more to explain away than those who accept it.

My dear friend, do you value the counsels of dead men?
I should say this. Fear defeat. Keep it before your minds
As much as victory. Defeat at the hands of friends,
Defeat in the plans of your confident generals.
Fear the kerchiefed captain who does not think he can die.

New prisoners bring news. The evening air unravels
The friendly scents from fruit trees, creepers and trellised
    vines.
In airless rooms, conversations are gently renewed.
An optimist licking his finger detects a breeze
And I begin to ignore the insidious voice

Which insists in whispers: The chance once lost is life lost
For the idea, for the losers and their dead
Whose memorials will never be honoured or built
Until they and those they have betrayed are forgotten –
Not this year, not next year, not in your time.

From 'Prison Island' by James Fenton
(*The Memory of War: Poems 1968–1982*)

These lines, from the best English poet of his time, have a certain ache to them. They have all the melancholy of remembered bravado and betrayal, as well as all the agony of loss and defeat. Yet they are, just, redeemed from utter despair. 'The insidious voice', which argues that an opportunity missed is the knell of finality, has to be heeded but answered – even, perhaps, resisted.

We are all prisoners of knowledge. To know how Cyprus was betrayed, and to have studied the record of that betrayal, is to make oneself unhappy and to spoil, perhaps for ever, one's pleasure in visiting one of the world's most enchanting islands. Nothing will ever restore the looted treasures, the bereaved families, the plundered villages and the groves and hillsides scalded with napalm. Nor will anything mitigate the record of the callous and crude politicians who regarded Cyprus as something on which to scribble their inane and conceited designs. But fatalism would be the worst betrayal of all. The acceptance, the legitimization of what was done – those things must be repudiated. Such a refusal has a value beyond Cyprus, in showing that acquiescence in injustice is not 'realism'. Once the injustice has been set down and described, and called by its right name, acquiescence in it becomes impossible. That is why one writes about Cyprus in sorrow but more – much more – in anger.

Appendix

Chronological Table of Events
(Reprinted by permission of Sir David Hunt and Sir Steven Runciman)

Early dates are very approximate only and between 4500 and 2500 B.C. they are obtained from calibrated radiocarbon (Carbon-14) determinations; earlier radiocarbon dates cannot yet be calibrated to calendrical dates but the earliest are likely to be far in excess (*c.* 1,000 years) of the quoted range.

B.C.

7000(?)–5300	NEOLITHIC (?) Colonization of Cyprus by farmers from Syria or Cilicia: deer herding(?)
5000–4000	Earliest pottery-using groups and signs of regionalization
4000–2500	CHALCOLITHIC Emergence of metal-users and settlement of west Cyprus
2700–1900	EARLY CYPRIOTE (EARLY BRONZE AGE) (Arrival of people from Anatolia; ox-plough cultivation starts; sporadic exchange with Levantine mainland)
1900–1600	MIDDLE CYPRIOTE (MIDDLE BRONZE AGE) Beginning of contacts with the Aegean
1900–1750	First mention of *Alasia* (probably Cyprus) and its export of copper in Near Eastern

	historical records
1650–	Start of large-scale pottery export to Levant and Egypt; fortifications and development of urbanization in Cyprus
1600–1050	LATE CYPRIOTE (LATE BRONZE AGE)
*c.*1500	Development of Enkomi as major port
*c.*1400	Large-scale imports of Mycenaean pottery begin
*c.*1375	References to Alashiya in Tel el-Amarna documents
*c.*1220	Enkomi and Kition destroyed by Sea Peoples; rebuilt shortly afterwards. First settlement at Maa-Palaeocastro
*c.*1190	Second settlement at Maa-Palaeocastro. Beginning of immigration of Achaeans. Fortification of Palaepaphos
*c.*1150	Second wave of Achaean settlers
*c.*1080	Third wave of Achaean settlers
*c.*1050	Enkomi abandoned
1050–950	CYPRO-GEOMETRIC I Consolidation of Cypriot kingdoms
950–850	CYPRO-GEOMETRIC II Obscure period
850–750	CYPRO-GEOMETRIC III Phoenician colony at Kition. Royal tombs at Salamis, first burials
750–600	CYPRO-ARCHAIC I
709	Seven Cypriot kings pay homage to Sargon II of Assyria
709–*c.*663	Assyrian domination
673/2	Ten Cypriot kings pay homage to Esarhaddon of Assyria
*c.*663–569	Cypriot kingdoms independent

600–475	CYPRO-ARCHAIC II
*c.*569	Amasis of Egypt takes control of Cyprus
*c.*569–545	Egyptian rule
560–525	Reign of Euelthon of Salamis
*c.*545	Cypriot kings transfer allegiance to Cyrus the Great, King of Persia; beginning of Persian domination
*c.*521	Included in the fifth satrapy of the Persian Empire under Darius
499	Outbreak of Ionian revolt against Persian rule; participation of all Cypriot cities except for Amathus, at the instigation of Onesilos, King of Salamis
498	Reduction of Cypriot cities
480	Battle of Salamis; Cyprus contributes 150 ships to the Persian fleet
475–400	CYPRO-CLASSICAL I
450–449	Cimon's expedition to liberate Cyprus from Persia
448	Peace of Callias; Cyprus left firmly under Persian control
411	Evagoras I becomes King of Salamis
400–325	CYPRO-CLASSICAL II
by 391	Evagoras I master of the whole of Cyprus
*c.*386	Peace of Antalcidas; Athens recognizes Persian sovereignty over Cyprus
*c.*381	Siege of Salamis by the Persians
380–379	Evagoras I loses control over Cypriot cities other than Salamis under a peace concluded with Persia
374/3	Murder of Evagoras I
351	Cypriot kings join Egypt and Phoenicia in revolt against Persia; siege of Salamis, revolt suppressed
*c.*335	Birth of Zeno, founder of Stoic school of philosophy, at Kition
*c.*333	End of Persian domination; Cypriot kings

	support Alexander the Great after his victory over the Persian forces at the battle of Issus
332	Cypriot ships take part in Alexander's naval siege of Tyre
331	Nicocreon becomes King of Salamis
325–150	HELLENISTIC I
323	Death of Alexander the Great; Cyprus becomes involved in struggles among his generals over the division of his empire
312	Certain Cypriot kings object to the rule of the general Ptolemy and are imprisoned or executed; Marion razed to the ground
310	Nicocreon, last king of Salamis, forced by Ptolemy to commit suicide. End of other city kingdoms
*c.*310	Zeno founds school of Stoic philosophy in Athens
305	Ptolemy proclaimed Ptolemy I Soter, King of Egypt
294	Annexation of Cyprus by Ptolemy I; Cyprus becomes part of the Hellenistic state of Egypt
*c.*264	Death of Zeno
168	Attack on Cyprus by Antiochus IV Epiphanes of Syria; withdrawal on intervention of Rome
150–30	HELLENISTIC II
*c.*106/5–88	Cyprus ruled as an independent kingdom by Lathyrus (Ptolemy IX Soter II) after his expulsion from Egypt
88	Lathyrus restored as King of Egypt
88–80	Cyprus returned to Egyptian rule
80	Death of Lathyrus. Ptolemies partly withdraw from Cyprus
80–58	Reign of Ptolemaios in Cyprus (brother of Ptolemy XII Auletes of Egypt)

58	Cyprus reduced to the state of a Roman province; suicide of Ptolemaios
*c.*47	Cyprus returned to Egyptian rule by Julius Caesar
30	Suicide of Cleopatra VII of Egypt; Cyprus finally becomes part of the Roman Empire
30–A.D. 300	THE ROMAN PERIOD
30 B.C.	Cyprus annexed by Augustus; forms part of province of Syria
22 B.C.	Cyprus a separate province under a proconsul
15 B.C.	Paphos almost completely destroyed by earthquake
A.D. 45	Missionary journey of SS Paul and Barnabas
47	Second missionary journey by SS Barnabas and Mark
76/77	Serious earthquake damage throughout Cyprus
116	Jewish insurrection
164	Heavy loss of life from plague
269	Raid by Goths
313	Edict of Milan grants freedom of worship to Christians
325	Cypriot bishops attend the council of Nicaea
330–1191	THE BYZANTINE PERIOD
330	Inauguration of Constantinople as capital of the Roman Empire
*c.*330	Empress Helena said to have visited Cyprus. Foundation of Stavrovouni Monastery
332	Paphos ruined by an earthquake
342	Salamis ruined by an earthquake and a tidal wave. Rebuilt as Constantia
431	Council of Ephesus. Cypriot Church given conditional autonomy
488	Discovery of relics of St Barnabas. Emperor Zeno gives Cypriot archbishop full autonomy and privileges

*c.*550	Establishment of silk industry in Cyprus
649	Arabs invade island under Muawiya. Death there of the lady Umm-Haram, cousin of the Prophet
653–4	Second Arab invasion. Arab garrison placed in Cyprus
688	Treaty between Emperor Justinian II and Caliph al-Malik neutralizing Cyprus
689	Numbers of Christian Cypriots moved to Bithynia
698	Cypriots in Bithynia return to Cyprus
723	English pilgrim Willibald visits the island
743	Arabs complain of breach of treaty and raid Cyprus
806	Raid on Cyprus ordered by Caliph Harun ar-Rashid
*c.*870–877	Temporary Byzantine occupation of the island
910	Byzantine admiral Himerius lands on island. His sailors molest Muslim villagers
912	Emir Damian of Tarsus raids island as a reprisal
965	Byzantines reoccupy Cyprus under Emperor Nicephorus Phocas. It becomes a province of the empire
1043	Unsuccessful revolt of Theophilus Eroticus, governor of the island
1093	Revolt of Cypriot governor Rhapsomates, put down by John Ducas and Butumites
1094	Monastery of Kykko founded by monk Isaias, under Butumites' patronage
*c.*1093–1100	Philocales Eustathius governs the island
*c.*1100–1105	Constantine Euphorbenus Catacalon, governor. Church at Asinou decorated under his patronage
1105–1112	Philocales Eustathius' second governorate
1099	Pisan fleet attempts unsuccessfully to raid the island

1157	Severe earthquake in Cyprus
1158	Egyptian fleet raids island
c.1170	St Neophytus founds monastery at Enkleistra
1185–1191	Isaac Ducas Comnenus takes over the government of the island and declares himself independent

1191–1192	RICHARD I (the Lionheart) AND TEMPLARS
1191	King Richard I of England defeats Isaac Comnenus and takes possession of Cyprus. He sells it to the Templars for 100,000 dinars. Richard marries Berengaria of Navarre in Limassol, where she is crowned Queen of England
1192	The Templars resell Cyprus to King Richard, who transfers it at the same price to Guy de Lusignan

1192–1571	THE FRANKISH PERIOD

1192–1489	THE LUSIGNAN DYNASTY
1192–1194	Guy de Lusignan, Lord of Cyprus
1194–1205	Aimery, brother of Guy, succeeds; he later obtains royal title from Emperor Henry VI
1197	Coronation of Aimery
1205–1218	Hugh I
1209	Foundation of Cathedral of Ayia Sophia in Nicosia
1217	Hugh I takes part in Fifth Crusade
1218–1253	Henry I
1220	Orthodox Archbishop and bishops replaced by Latins
1228	Emperor Frederick II in Cyprus; he is recognized as suzerain
1229	Frederick II returns to West; rising of Cypriot barons against his deputies
1232	Battle of Aghirda. Imperialists defeated

1233	Imperialist garrison of Kyrenia capitulates
1249	Henry I takes part in Seventh Crusade
1253–1267	Hugh II
	Plaisance of Antioch acts as Regent until 1261
1260	Orthodox Church in Cyprus subordinated to Latin Church by Papal Bull (Bulla Cypria)
1261	Hugh of Antioch Regent; becomes king on death of Hugh II
1267–1284	Hugh III
1284–1285	John I
1285–1324	Henry II
1291	Fall of Acre and extinction of Latin rule in Syria
1306	Henry II's brother Amaury usurps power
1310	Henry II exiled to Cilicia; returns after murder of Amaury
1324–1358	Hugh IV
1350	Consecration of Orthodox Church of Phaneromeni
1359–1369	Peter I
1361	Capture of Adalia
1362–1365	Peter I travels in West to obtain support for new Crusade
1365	Sack of Alexandria
1369–1382	Peter II
1372	Rioting between Venetians and Genoese in Famagusta
1373–1374	War with Genoa. Cyprus agrees to large indemnity and cession of Famagusta
1382–1398	James I (prisoner in Genoa at accession)
1385	James I released by Genoese and crowned in Nicosia
1393	Assumes title of King of Armenia
1398–1432	Janus
1426	Invasion of Cyprus by Egyptians. Janus defeated and taken prisoner at battle of Khirokitia
1427	Janus ransomed and returns to Cyprus

1432–1458	John II
1441	John II marries Helena Palaeologina, daughter of Despot of the Morea
1458–1460	Charlotte, Queen of Cyprus
1460–1473	James II
1464	James expels Genoese from Famagusta
1472	James marries Catherine Cornaro (married by proxy in 1468)
1473–1474	James II, posthumous child of James II and Catherine
1474–1489	Catherine Cornaro Queen of Cyprus
1479	Conspiracy against Catherine in favour of King of Naples suppressed
1489	Catherine cedes Cyprus to the Venetian state
1489–1571	THE VENETIAN PERIOD
1510	Death of Catherine
1517	Ottoman Sultan, having conquered Egypt, becomes Suzerain of Cyprus
1562	Conspiracy of Greek Cypriots against Venetian rule
1566	Accession of Sultan Selim
1570	Turkish invasion force lands. Capture of Nicosia. Siege of Famagusta begins
1571	Famagusta capitulates to Turkish commander Lala Mustafa. Breach of capitulation by Turks. Cyprus annexed to Ottoman Empire
1571–1878	THE TURKISH PERIOD
1572	Expulsion of Latin hierarchy and restoration of Orthodox
1578	Mutinous Turkish troops kill the governor Arab Ahmet Pasha
1641	Suppression of Pashaliks of Paphos and Famagusta
1670	Cyprus downgraded from Pashalik and put under Kapudan Pasha
1673	Rebellion of Mehmed Agha Boyajioglou

1680	Boyajioglou executed
1703	Cyprus transferred to direct jurisdiction of Grand Vizier
1745	Cyprus removed from Grand Vizier and created an independent Pashalik again
1746–1748	Abu Bekr Pasha, only well-regarded governor
1751	Cyprus returned to direct jurisdiction of Grand Vizier
1754	Archbishop and Orthodox hierarchy made responsible for collecting taxes
1764	Chil Osman Agha appointed governor. After more than doubling taxes he is killed in revolt
1765–1766	Revolt of Khalil Agha, Commandant of Kyrenia
1777–1783	Hali Baki Agha governor
1820–1822	Küchük Mehmed governor
1821	Execution of Archbishop Kyprianos and three bishops
1833	Insurrection of Ibrahim of Paphos, known as Giaur Imam
1849	Cyprus included in Pashalik of Archipelago
1856	Government takes over collection of taxes from Archbishop
1861	Cyprus an independent province
1868–1871	Cyprus put under vilayet of Dardanelles
1871	Cyprus put under vilayet of Archipelago
1878–1960	THE BRITISH PERIOD
1878	Under the Cyprus Convention Britain assumes administration of the island which remains formally part of Ottoman Empire. Sir Garnet Wolseley first High Commissioner
1880	Greek established as medium of education (Turkish in Turkish schools)
1881	Administrative supervision transferred from Foreign Office to Colonial Office

1883	First meeting of elected advisory Council
1908	Riots in Nicosia over election of Archbishop
1914	Cyprus annexed by Britain in consequence of outbreak of war with Turkey
1924	Under Treaty of Lausanne Turkey renounces claim to Cyprus in favour of Britain
1931	Greek elected members resign from the Legislative Council; pro-*enosis* riots in Nicosia; Government House is burned down; Constitution suspended
1941	Prohibition on political parties rescinded
1947	Lord Winster appointed Governor; his proposals, including an elected legislature, rejected
1948	Elections for a consultative Assembly are boycotted
1949	Ethnarchic Council created under Archbishop Makarios II. All parties represented on it
1950	Plebiscite of Greek Cypriots, organized by Archbishop, shows ninety-six per cent in favour of *enosis*; election as Archbishop of Makarios III
1954	Further British proposal for a legislative Council is rejected; frustration of first appeal to UN by Greece leads to strikes in Cyprus
1955	(April 1) Campaign in favour of *enosis* started by EOKA under Grivas, code-name 'Dighenis'; a state of emergency is declared; tripartite conference in London
1955–1957	Sir John Harding (later Lord Harding of Petherton) Governor
1956	Archbishop Makarios exiled to the Seychelles
1957	Radcliffe proposals rejected; Turkish Cypriots declare for Federation or partition; Makarios released from the Seychelles but banned from Cyprus

1957–1960	Sir Hugh Foot (later Lord Caradon) Governor
1958	Zurich Agreement between Greece and Turkey
1959	(January) London Conference (Greece, Turkey, UK, Greek Cypriots, Turkish Cypriots) agrees on independence of Cyprus; (March) Makarios returns to Cyprus; (December) Makarios elected President and Dr Fazil Kuchuk Vice President
1960	INDEPENDENT REPUBLIC
1960	(July) General elections to House of Representatives; (16 August) Cyprus becomes an independent republic
1961	Agreement on British Sovereign Bases signed
1963	(December) Outbreak of intercommunal fighting; 'Green Line' dividing communities in Nicosia established
1964	(January) Announcement by Dr Kuchuk in favour of partition; (March) Security Council resolution in support of Cyprus sovereignty denounces threat or use of force; arrival of UNFICYP; (May) conscription is introduced; (June) Grivas returns and assumes command of Cyprus National Guard
1965	(March) Galo Plaza, UN Mediator, publishes report and proposals; rejected by Turkish government
1966	(February) Joint communiqué signed by the governments of Cyprus and Greece that any solution excluding *enosis* would be unacceptable
1967	(April) Military coup in Greece; (November) fighting between National Guard under Grivas and Turkish Cypriots in Kophinou area leads to Turkish ultimatum;

	accepted by Greek junta which withdraws troops, and Grivas, from Cyprus; (December) Turkish Cypriots announce formation of 'Provisional Cyprus–Turkish Administration'
1971	Grivas returns secretly to Cyprus; start of renewed campaign for *enosis* by EOKA-B
1974	(January) Death of Grivas; (July) Makarios demands withdrawal of Greek officers; (15 July) conspiracy against Makarios inspired by Greek junta; Presidential Palace destroyed; Nikos Sampson declared President; (20 July) start of Turkish invasion; (23 July) Glafkos Clerides Acting President; (7 December) Makarios returns
1975	Start of intercommunal talks, in first place in Vienna
1977	(January) Meeting between Makarios and Denktash; (3 August) death of Makarios; succeeded as President by Spyros Kyprianou, as Archbishop by Chrysostomos, Bishop of Paphos
1978	(January) President Kyprianou returned unopposed for five-year term
1981	Elections for House of Representatives under new electoral system (reinforced representational)
1982	Greek Prime Minister, Andreas Papandreou, pays official visit to Cyprus
1983	Turkish State of North Kibris proclaimed

Select Bibliography

The following list is selective and individual. Many of the most important findings about Cyprus occur in books on other topics. The reader in search of a comprehensive bibliography is referred to *Cyprus*, compiled by Paschalis Kitromilides and Marios Evriviades and published by Clio Press, Oxford and Santa Barbara, in 1982. Below are books which I have found indispensable, and to which I acknowledge a debt.

Doros Alastos, *Cyprus in History* (Zeno Publishers, London, 1955)

Michael Attalides, *Cyprus* (Q Press, Edinburgh, 1979)

Mehmet Ali Birand, *Thirty Hot Days in Cyprus* (Istanbul, 1976)

Van Coufoudakis, *Essays on the Cyprus Conflict* (Pella Publishing, 1976)

Theodore Couloumbis and Sally Hicks (eds), *US Foreign Policy Toward Greece and Cyprus* (Conference Proceedings, Center for Mediterranean Studies and American Hellenic Institute, Washington, 1975)

Nancy Crawshaw, *The Cyprus Revolt* (George Allen and Unwin, 1978)

European Commission of Human Rights, *Report of the Commission* (Council of Europe. Applications Nos 6780/74 and 6950/75. Cyprus Against Turkey. Adopted 10 July 1976)

Charles Foley, *Island in Revolt* (Longman's, London, 1962)

Hugh Foot, *A Start in Freedom* (Hodder and Stoughton, London, 1964)

Seymour Hersh, *The Price of Power: Kissinger in the Nixon White House* (Summit Books, London, 1983)

Sir George Hill, *A History of Cyprus* (4 Vols) (Cambridge University Press, Cambridge, 1940–52)

Sir David Hunt (ed.), *Footprints in Cyprus* (Trigraph, 1982)

Stanley Kyriakides, *Cyprus, Constitutionalism and Crisis Government* (University of Pennsylvania, 1968)

C.W.J. Orr, *Cyprus under British Rule* (Zeno Publishers, London, 1972)

Andreas Papandreou, *Democracy at Gunpoint* (André Deutsch, London, 1971)

Polyvios Polyviou, *Cyprus, The Tragedy and the Challenge* (1975); *Cyprus in Search of a Constitution* (1976); *Cyprus, Conflict and Negotiation* (Duckworth, London, 1980)

Robert Stephens, *Cyprus: a Place of Arms* (Pall Mall Press, 1966)

Laurence Stern, *The Wrong Horse* (*Times Books*, New York, 1977)

Frank G. Weber, *The Evasive Neutral* (University of Missouri, 1979)

Lawrence S. Wittner, *American Intervention in Greece 1943–1949* (Columbia University Press, 1982)

C.M. Woodhouse, *Something Ventured* (Granada, London, 1982)

Index